Advance praise for

The No-Cry Sleep Solution

"Humane, sensitive, and baby-centered. It is refreshing to see and
to be able to endorse an approach toward tender infant and
child caregiving that does not claim to know who and what
every baby should be or what every parent should do to achieve
parenting success. *The No-Cry Sleep Solution* speaks to the
uniqueness of each parent and child in a loving and knowl-
edgeable way."

—James J. McKenna, Ph.D., Director, Mother Baby
Behavioral Sleep Center, University of Notre Dame

"A wise and wonderful answer to every tired parent's prayers.
Finally, a sleep solution that is loving, gentle, intuitive, safe, and
successful. Elizabeth Pantley teaches parents how to build, step
by step, a pleasurable nighttime experience without the restric-
tions that have turned parents away from sleep advice. *The No-
Cry Sleep Solution* should be a part of every prenatal and baby
class!"

—Nancy Eggleston, Community Producer, StorkNet.com

"Offers a marvelous balance between acknowledging the mean-
ingfulness of infant crying and recognizing the reality of parents'
exhaustion. Parents will find confirmation of their suspicion that
the crying of babies should not be ignored and affirmation of
their own power to help their baby learn how to sleep."

—Michael Trout, Director, The Infant-Parent Institute, Inc.

"At long last, a book that deals sensitively with a sensitive issue: how to get babies to sleep without resorting to letting them 'cry it out.' If you are one of those parents who stumbles through your days groggy and cranky after seemingly endless nights with a sleepless baby or toddler, or if you are simply a parent who would like to prevent that scenario, this is the book to read. It offers real-life, workable answers to one of the most challenging and confusing situations that parents face."
—*Tricia Jalbert and Macall Gordon, Executive Editors,*
Attachment Parenting International

"It has always bothered me that every 'sleep through' method touted by so-called experts was *cruel* to babies and young children. Elizabeth Pantley has answered the sleepy prayers of parents all over the world and provided a sensitive and caring method that actually works! To all the tired parents out there: This is the book of your dreams!"
—*Gaye E. Ward, Founder, Gayesy's Attachment Parenting*

"Finally! A book to help all parents gently and lovingly guide their babies to better sleep. Elizabeth's techniques and approaches are an excellent way to encourage a child into a healthy sleeping schedule. This fantastic book is for everyone, regardless of parenting style, feeding situation, or sleeping arrangement."
—*Tammy Frissell-Deppe, Author,*
Every Parent's Guide to Attachment Parenting,
GetAttached.com

"Clearly stated, without guilt trips or shortcuts, this book is as pleasurable as it is helpful. The bond that you will develop with your baby as together you overcome the sleepless nights, and the insight that you will acquire by adhering to Pantley's program, will no doubt prove an asset for years to come, enhancing your ability to positively influence your child's development. This book goes way beyond its stated goal. In short, it's a must."

—*Richard Rubin, Editor, Baby-Place.com*

"Finally, a gentle, loving answer to baby sleep woes. Elizabeth Pantley's suggestions make sense—and they work! In this positive and practical guide, she demonstrates how understanding your baby's innate needs and learned responses will help you work together to get the soothing rest you all need."

—*Nancy Price, Cofounder, Myria Network: Myria.com,*
ePregnancy.com, GeoParent.com

"Whether Baby sleeps in a crib or the family bed, *The No-Cry Sleep Solution* is full of supportive, encouraging, and sensible ideas that respect the needs of both baby and parents. The book reflects the fact that each family is unique and requires more than a one-size-fits-all solution to sleep issues. Parents will welcome Elizabeth Pantley's empathetic insight and parenting experience."

—*Judy Arnall, Founder,*
Whole Family Attachment Parenting Association

the no-cry sleep solution

*Gentle Ways to Help Your Baby
Sleep Through the Night*

Elizabeth Pantley

New York Chicago San Francisco Lisbon London Madrid Mexico City
Milan New Delhi San Juan Seoul Singapore Sydney Toronto

The **McGraw·Hill** Companies

Library of Congress Cataloging-in-Publication Data

Pantley, Elizabeth.
    The no-cry sleep solution : gentle ways to help your baby sleep through the
night / Elizabeth Pantley.
        p.   cm.
    Includes index.
    ISBN 0-07-138139-2
    1. Infants (Newborn)—Sleep.   2. Sleep disorders in children.
3. Parent and child.   4. Child rearing.   I. Title.

RJ506.S55 P36   2002
618.92'8498—dc21   2001047721

28 29 30 31 32 33 34 35   DOC/DOC   1 9 8 7 6 5 4 3 2 1

ISBN 978-0-07-138139-0
MHID   0-07-138139-2

Cover and interior design by Nick Panos
Front-cover photograph copyright © Elizabeth Hathon/corbisstockmarket.com
Back-cover photograph by Yuen Lui Studios

McGraw-Hill books are available at special quantity discounts to use as premiums and
sales promotions or for use in corporate training programs. To contact a representative,
please e-mail us at bulksales@mcgraw-hill.com.

This book is dedicated to my husband, Robert, for all the things you do as father to our children—things that may sometimes seem insignificant but are the pieces of life I cherish most in the special place in my heart that only you know. This book is for you, my husband, for:

Wrapping our first child, Angela, in her very first diaper. Your delicate and vigilant movements that day make this the memory I cherish most from my first moments as a mother.

Carrying newborn Vanessa in a sling as we shopped the mall. For placing your hand under her diminutive body as you walked, for peeking at her face between sentences, and for that look of love and pride that glowed in your eyes.

Singing to David all those silly songs that made him laugh. And singing them with as much gusto and emotion the tenth time around as you had the first.

Rocking baby Coleton to sleep, even when your arms fell asleep before he did. And for never, ever ignoring a call of "Daddy" from a toddling little boy, no matter how busy you are.

Coaching our children and others in softball, with a heart as big as all the world. For the day when the opposing pitcher struggled on the mound and broke down in tears: How can I forget the scene as you emerged from the dugout with a box of tissue and draped your arm around her shoulder, encouraging her to finish the game?

Guiding our children in their studies with the perfect balance of seriousness (those goal-setting meetings) and fun (helping with homework while eating popcorn and watching the Mariners play baseball).

Inviting child after child into our home. And then, when your invitation includes the entire softball team to sleep over, staying up late so I can go to bed early.

Teaching the importance of thoughtfulness, caring, and family by hugging Grama when she most needs a hug, surprising her when she most needs a surprise, and saying "thank you" for every deed great or small.

Revealing to our children the secrets of a long and lasting marriage—trust, honesty, respect, and affection—so that they may emulate ours and grow up to cherish marriages of their own.

Understanding that our baby's bedtime ritual takes precedence over dinner parties; that a perfect French braid is as important as getting to the field on time; that breakfast out with Daddy on Sunday morning is an essential ingredient to a happy childhood; and that a closed door to a teenager's room sometimes represents a more earnest invitation than an open one.

Recognizing that "Daddy" is your most significant title in life right now and maybe, just maybe, for always.

Contents

Foreword

Sleep—or more accurately, the *lack* of sleep—is one of the most challenging aspects of parenting during the first year or two of a baby's life. The biggest hurdle is getting the baby to sleep through the night. Parents who are sensitive to their baby's needs are reluctant to try any technique that requires that they let their baby cry, so they often struggle through a fog of sleeplessness. This "nighttime-martyr parenting" often leads to frustration and resentment, resulting in unnecessary feelings of guilt and obscuring a family's joy over the new arrival. At a time when new parents should be enjoying the process of getting to know their baby, this lack of sleep leaves parents doubting themselves.

I've always thought that it would be wonderful to have a menu of ideas that parents could try until they hit upon a magic antidote to help their baby sleep all night. Elizabeth Pantley has created just such a menu in *The No-Cry Sleep Solution*.

The beauty of this book is that parents can create their very own sleep plan based on their baby's makeup as well as their own. Parents can choose from a variety of sensible, sensitive solutions that respect both baby and parent, striking a balance between a baby's nighttime requirements and the parents' very real need for a full night's sleep. The ideas are firmly rooted in the concept that the early years are the time to help your child develop a healthy sleep attitude—one that regards sleep as a pleasant, peaceful, necessary state that's not to be feared.

You've most likely picked up this book because your baby is keeping you up all night. Your lack of sleep has probably affected your ability to function fully throughout the day. Elizabeth Pantley, an experienced mother of four, clearly understands where you sit today, having sat there herself on occasion. She's created a book that is clear, easy to read, and uncomplicated. The steps are set up so that even the most sleep-deprived can understand and apply the solutions.

At long last, I've found a book that I can hand to weary parents with the confidence that they can learn to help their baby sleep through the night—without the baby crying it out.

—*William Sears, M.D.*

A Note from Author Elizabeth Pantley

Dr. Sears is my parenting hero. His books came to my aid when I was a nervous and inexperienced new mother fourteen years ago. His wisdom and knowledge helped me learn what it really means to be a parent, and his gentle insight showed me how to do the job in the most loving and successful way. I am deeply honored that he finds my books so helpful to parents that he is willing to write the foreword for each one. My perception is that most parents know Dr. Sears—and those who don't, should.

Dr. Sears is one of America's most acclaimed and respected pediatricians, an associate clinical professor of pediatrics at the University of California School of Medicine. He is the pediatric and parenting expert for Parenting.com as well as his own website, AskDrSears.com. He and his wife, Martha Sears, R.N., are the parents of eight children and the grandparents of four. They appear frequently on national television, are extensively quoted in the media, and are the authors or collaborators of thirty parenting books, all of which I enthusiastically recommend. A partial list of Dr. Sears's work includes *The Attachment Parenting Book*, *The Baby Book*, *The Successful Child*, *The Discipline Book*, and *Nighttime Parenting*.

Acknowledgments

I am very grateful for the support of the many people who have made this book possible, and I would like to express my sincere appreciation to:

Judith McCarthy at McGraw-Hill/Contemporary Books—thank you for your unwavering support and guidance.

Meredith Bernstein of Meredith Bernstein Literary Agency, New York—thank you for your high-energy enthusiasm and your ability to get things done.

Vanessa Sands—thank you for sharing your insight, talent, and friendship.

Pia Davis, Christine Galloway, and Kim Crowder—thank you for lending your experience as successful test mommies to the final material.

My test mommies: Alice, Alison, Amber, Andrea, Ann, Annette, Becca, Becky, Bilquis, Carol, Caryn, Christine C., Christine Ga., Christine Gr., Cindy, Dana, Dayna, Deirdre, Diane, Elaine, Elvina, Emily, Gloria, Jenn, Jenny, Jessie, Jill, Julie, Kari, Kelly, Kim, Kristene, Lauren, Lesa B., Leesa H., Lisa Ab., Lisa As., Lisa G., Lorelie, Marsha, Melanie, Neela, Pam, Penny, Pia, Rene, Robin, Sandy, Shannon R., Shannon J., Sharon, Shay, Staci, Susan, Suzanne, Tammy, Tanya, Tina, Victoria, and Yelena—thank you for every comment and every question along the way. (Give all your babies a hug from me.)

Judy Arnall, Maribeth Doerr, Nancy Eggleston, Tammy Frissel-Deppe, Macall Gordon, Tricia Jalbert, Dr. James J. McKenna, Nancy Price, Richard Rubin, Michael Trout, and Gaye E. Ward—thank you for your enthusiastic and encouraging support.

Dolores Feldman, my mom—thank you for being a blessing in my life, every day. I love you.

Introduction

Do any of these describe your baby?

- It takes *forever* to get my baby to fall asleep.
- My baby will only fall asleep if I do one or more of the following: breastfeed, bottle-feed, give a pacifier, rock, carry, swing, or take a ride in the car.
- My baby wakes up frequently throughout the night.
- My baby won't nap easily, or takes very short naps.

Does this describe you?

- I desperately want my baby to sleep better.
- I won't—I can't—let my baby cry it out.

If so, this book is written for you. It will explain the exact steps you can take to gently help your baby sleep through the night. So, prop your eyelids open, grab a cup of coffee, and let me explain how you can help your baby sleep—so that *you* can get some sleep, too.

How do I know so much about children and sleep? I am the proud and lucky mother of four children who shine the light on my life, whether they're asleep or awake. There's firstborn Angela, now fourteen, and leading me into the (so far) delightful experience of mothering a teenager. Not far behind her are twelve-year-old Vanessa and ten-year-old David. And then there's two-year-old Coleton. Ahh, Coleton. Our little surprise treasure who reminded me of all the wonderful things I love about babies. And who also reminded me that with babies . . . come sleepless nights.

With two of my children, I would not have needed this book. David followed such a textbook pattern of sleep that I barely remember that time in our lives. Vanessa was one of those *very* unusual babies who, miraculously, was sleeping ten straight hours by the time she was six weeks old. (I wouldn't believe it myself if it were not written in her baby book!) My oldest and my youngest, though, were frequent night wakers. While I was in the process of convincing Coleton, my youngest, to go to sleep at bedtime—and *stay* asleep, *all* night—I discovered many wonderful, practical, loving solutions to my problem. As an author and parent educator, I take pleasure in sharing these with you in hopes that you'll get some shut-eye, too.

How This Book Will Help You

Through months of research, personal experience, and work with test case families, I have assembled and organized a wide variety of gentle ideas into what I call the No-Cry Sleep Solution. It's a ten-step plan to help your baby sleep through the night. It's not a rigid, unpleasant process. It does not involve letting your baby cry—not even for a minute. Rather, it consists of a customized plan that you create for your own family based on the ideas and research I present here, all within a simple and easy-to-follow framework. It's a method that is as gentle and loving as it is effective. Let me first tell you why I became passionate about writing this book.

Fourteen years ago, when Angela was a baby, I faced your dilemma. She did not sleep through the night. On the contrary, she woke up every two hours for my attention. As a new and inexperienced parent, I searched for solutions in books, articles, and conversations with other parents.

I soon discovered two basic schools of thought when it comes to babies and sleep. One side advocates letting a baby cry until she learns to fall asleep on her own. The other side says that it is

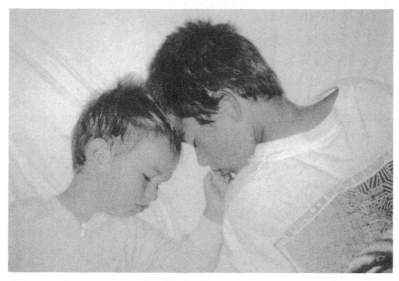

Coleton, eighteen months old, and David, nine years old

normal for babies to wake up at night and that it is a parent's job to nurture the baby—all day and all night. Eventually, when your baby is ready, she will sleep through the night.

In a nutshell, the two methods can be summed up as "cry it out" or "live with it." I wanted neither. I knew there had to be a kinder way, a road somewhere between nighttime neglect and daytime exhaustion that would be nurturing for my baby *and* for me.

Those many years ago, after all of my research about babies and their fragile needs, I felt guilty and selfish when I began to wish for an uninterrupted night's sleep. It was nearly impossible to reconcile my own instincts regarding Angela's nighttime needs with the fatigue that hampered my daytime parenting. Time passed, and eventually my daughter did sleep through the night—but not until after her second birthday.

Cry It Out

Cry-it-out advocates make it sound so easy. A few nights of crying, and your baby will be sleeping all night, every night. If only it *were* so simple! My research has shown that very few parents experience this effortless success. Many deal with weeks of crying for hours each night (for baby *and* parent, in many instances). Some babies cry so violently that they vomit. Some parents find that the nighttime crying affects their baby's daytime personality—making him clingy and fussy. Many find that any setback (teething, sickness, missing a nap, going on vacation) sends them back to the previous night-waking problems, and they must let the child cry it out over and over again. Many (if not all) parents who resort to letting their baby cry it out do so because they believe that it is the only way they will get their baby to sleep through the night.

My Personal Experience with Cry It Out

At one point during Angela's period of sleeplessness I *did* cave in to all the pressure from friends, family, and even my pediatrician, who recommended that a few nights of crying would solve our problem. (If you're reading this book, you know this pressure, too.) So one dreadful night, I let her cry it out.

Oh, I checked on her often enough, each time increasing the length of time before I returned to her side. But each return visit struck me with my precious baby holding out her arms, desperately and helplessly crying, "Mama!" with a look of terror and confusion on her tiny face. And *sobbing*. After two hours of this torment, I was crying, too.

I picked up my cherished baby and held her tightly in my arms. She was too distraught to nurse, too distressed to sleep. I held her and kissed her downy head as her body shook and hiccuped in the aftermath of her sobbing. I thought, "This approach is responding to a child's needs? This is teaching her that her world is worthy of her faith and trust? *This is nurturing?*"

I decided then and there: they are all wrong. Horribly, intolerably, painfully wrong. I was convinced that this was a simplistic and harsh way to treat another human being, let alone the precious little love of my life. To allow a baby to suffer through pain and fear until she resigns herself to sleep is heartless and, for me, unthinkable.

I promised my baby that I would never again follow the path that *others* prescribed for us. I would never again allow her to cry it out. Even more, I vowed not to let any of her brothers or sisters-to-be suffer the horrible experience we'd just endured.

And I never have.

Thirteen Years Later: The More Things Change . . .

At twelve months old, my fourth baby, Coleton, was not sleeping through the night. Following in his older sister's footsteps, and *beating* her record, he was waking up nearly every hour for my attention. Now a mature, seasoned parent and professional parent educator, I found that my beliefs about letting a baby cry it out had not changed at all. But knowing that so many other parents feel the same way, I was certain that the intervening years would have produced new solutions. I thought I would find useful, concrete ideas in a book, and I began my search.

Nearly a month later, eyes glazed over with fatigue, I evaluated my finds. Before me sat a stack of articles and books—old and new—with the same two choices to address my dilemma: either let the baby cry it out or learn to live with it.

What Experts Say About the Mutual Agony of the Cry-It-Out Method

I *did* find a lot of new data that reinforced my abhorrence of letting a baby cry it out. Dr. Paul M. Fleiss and Frederick Hodges in *Sweet Dreams* (Lowell House, 2000) have this to say about such training programs for babies:

> Babies and young children are emotional rather than rational creatures. A child cannot comprehend why you are ignoring his cries for help. Ignoring your baby's cries, even with the best of intentions, may lead him to feel that he has been abandoned. Babies are responding to biological needs that sleep "experts" either ignore or deny. It is true that a baby whose crying is ignored may eventually fall back asleep, but the problem that caused the night waking in the first place has remain unsolved. Even if parents have checked to make sure that the baby is not sick or in physical discomfort, unless they pick up the baby, interact with him in a compassionate way, soothe him, or nurse him until he falls back asleep, the underlying or accompanying emotional stress will remain.
>
> The most sensible and compassionate approach is to respond immediately to your child's cries. Remind yourself that you are the parent, and that giving your baby reassurance is one of the joyous responsibilities of being a parent. It is a beautiful feeling knowing that you alone have the power to brighten your child's life and banish fear and sorrow.

Kate Allison Granju, in *Attachment Parenting* (Pocket Books, 1999), writes:

> Babies are people, extremely helpless, vulnerable, and dependent people. Your baby counts on you to lovingly care for her. When she cries, she is signaling—in the only way she knows how—that she needs you to be with her.

You know what it feels like to cry in fear or distress. It feels terrible. And it's no different for your baby. When your baby cries—for whatever reason—he experiences physical changes. His blood pressure rises, his muscles become tense, and stress hormones flood his little body.

Babies who are subjected to cry-it-out sleep training do sometimes seem to sleep deeply after they finally drop off. This is because babies and young children frequently sleep deeply after experiencing trauma. This deep sleep shouldn't be viewed as proof of the efficacy of the [cry-it-out] method but rather evidence of one of its many disturbing shortcomings.

Dr. William Sears, in *Nighttime Parenting* (Plume, 1999), says that letting a baby cry it out creates "detachment parenting" and goes so far as to warn parents against this approach. "Parents, let me caution you. Difficult problems in child rearing do not have easy answers. Children are too valuable and their needs too important to be made victims of cheap, shallow advice."

What Other Parents Have to Say About the Cry-It-Out Approach

As I spoke with parents about this new book, many came forward to share their personal experiences with letting their babies cry it out.

"When we tried letting Christoph cry it out, he cried for two or three hours every night for eleven nights in a row. He became fearful and fussy all day long. Since we gave up that awful idea, we've all been sleeping better."

—*Amy, mother of ten-month-old Christoph*

"We tried letting Emily cry herself to sleep when she was nine months old. It worked for a few days, and I got really excited. But then she went right back to her old pattern. It's never worked since."

—Christine, mother of eighteen-month-old Emily

"With my first child, I worried about doing things the 'right' way and so I tried to do cry-it-out sleep training. I discovered that there are so many relapses even after doing it—traveling, sicknesses, bad dreams, new situations, etc., etc., etc.—that it wasn't worth it to do it in the first place. Doing it once was bad enough; I couldn't stomach multiple cry-it-out sessions."

—Heather, mother of fifteen-month-old Anna
and three-year-old Brandon

"We tried the cry-it-out method; our pediatrician told me to just let him cry all night if necessary. Well, he cried off and on for four hours, slept until 2:30 A.M., and then cried off and on until I got him up at 6 A.M. It was absolute torture! I found the 'crying' part of the idea works, but there was no 'sleeping' for either of us."

—Silvana, mother of nine-month-old Salvador

"With our firstborn, we dutifully worked at getting her to sleep in her crib and finally did let her cry, believing we were doing the right thing. It was not the right answer for her at all. At one point, she cried for more than an hour and was literally foaming at the mouth. I was so sick over this and (obviously) still feel bad about it. From that point on, she slept with us. She is almost three now and sleeps well in her own bed. If she has a nightmare, she is welcomed into our bed. I am currently breastfeeding and co-sleeping with our son. He is not the best sleeper, but I feel strongly that my parenting does not end at night, and if crying is the only solution I'm not interested."

—*Rachel, mother of ten-month-old Jean-Paul and three-year-old Angelique*

How Does a Baby Feel About Crying It Out?

No one can really tell us how a baby feels about crying to sleep, but many people guess—taking advantage of a baby's lack of voice to present their own case. In my research for this book, I viewed a video by a sleep "expert" who stated, "Letting your baby cry herself to sleep is not physically or physiologically harmful, even if she cries for hours." This apparently is his rationalization to make parents feel better about letting their baby cry. I was so appalled that I immediately conveyed this information to my husband, who is a caring, supportive, and involved father to our children. The statement haunted him so much that he responded the next morning via E-mail with his answer to any parent who hears this advice:

> If you believe what this "expert" says then you are going down the wrong road with your child. Don't think for a minute that your tiny baby is not affected by this attitude. This insensitivity to your child's feelings can be born here and bred into other areas as he grows. If he wants you to hold him during the day, and you're too busy with other things, you can convince yourself that he won't be permanently harmed by your inattention. As he gets older, when he wants to play ball with you but you're otherwise occupied, you can rationalize that he's better off playing with his friends. If he wants you to attend a school function and you are too tired, you can argue that your presence really isn't necessary. You are setting up a pattern in babyhood

that will follow for the rest of your life in your relationship with your child. There are times to encourage independence in your children, but parents should choose those times with wisdom.

On that same video, the author offers this terrifying statement to sleep-deprived parents. "She will *never* learn to fall asleep unless you let her cry." Really? Tell this to my four children who now sleep through the night. Tell this to the millions of babies who *do* eventually sleep through the night without ever having to cry it out.

No one truly knows how crying it out affects a baby in the long run. After all, one cannot raise a baby twice and note the difference. And no one really knows how a baby feels when he is left to cry it out. Jean Liedloff presents a very likely perception in her volume on anthropology, *The Continuum Concept* (Addison-Wesley, 1977). Here, she describes a baby waking in the middle of the night:

> He awakes in a mindless terror of the silence, the motionlessness. He screams. He is afire from head to foot with want, with desire, with intolerable impatience. He gasps for breath and screams until his head is filled and throbbing with the sound. He screams until his chest aches, until his throat is sore. He can bear the pain no more and his sobs weaken and subside. He listens. He opens and closes his fists. He rolls his head from side to side. Nothing helps. It is unbearable. He begins to cry again, but it is too much for his strained throat; he soon stops. He waves his hands and kicks his feet. He stops, able to suffer, unable to think, unable to hope. He listens. Then he falls asleep again.

Renewed Resolve, but Tired Nonetheless

So, reading all these books had strengthened my resolve *not* to let my baby cry himself to sleep. Nevertheless, with the perspective of experience—as a mother of four—I refused to feel guilty for wanting a good night's sleep. I wanted sleep. I wanted answers.

There *had* to be answers.

My research began in earnest. I searched the library and bookstores, and I took to the Internet. Predictably, I found abundant articles and stories on babies and sleep. Observations and laments were easy to come by. But solutions? The same two schools of thought appeared over and over: cry it out or live with it.

Parents, though, seemed to fall into only one main category: sleep-deprived and desperate. Here's how Leesa, mother of nine-month-old Kyra, described her condition:

> I am truly distressed, as the lack of sleep is starting to affect all aspects of my life. I feel as though I can't carry on an intelligent conversation. I am extremely disorganized and don't have the energy to even attempt reorganization. I love this child more than anything in the world, and I don't want to make her cry, but I'm near tears myself thinking about going to bed every night. Sometimes I think, "What's the point? I'll just be up in an hour anyway." My husband keeps turning to me for answers, and I'm to the point where I nearly yell at him, "If I knew the answers, wouldn't Kyra be sleeping?!"

At this point in my own research, I began thinking that other parents going through the frequent night-waking ordeal would have ideas to share. So I sought out parenting websites with posting boards and chat lines, finding a multitude of parents facing the nightly crying versus grin-and-bear-it decision. And there, in the bits and pieces of conversations that quoted personal experience, articles, books, and other sources, along with my own experimentations with my little Coleton, I began to find solutions. There, in personal experience, and in the interpersonal exchanges between parents who have tried every conceivable method, I began to find ideas that did not sentence a baby to hours of nightly crying. I found the solutions that offered more peaceful paths to the rest so desperately needed by the whole family.

I researched the scientific reasons that babies wake up at night and dissected truth from fallacy. I picked apart the myriad solutions I'd read about, immersed myself in whatever I could find on the subject, and kept in regular contact with other sleep-deprived parents. Slowly, from the middle ground between the misery of the cry-it-out method and the quiet fatigue of all-night parenting, rose a plan—a gentle, nurturing plan to help my baby sleep.

I Know Because I've Been There

Most books on babies and sleep are written by experts who—while well-versed in the technical and physiological aspects of sleep—simply and obviously don't have a personal understanding of the agony of being kept up all night—night after night—by their babies or the heartache of hearing their little ones cry for them in the darkness. In contrast, I've experienced the foggy existence of sleepless nights. And having four unique children has afforded me the insight that, while it is *possible* for a very young baby to sleep all night, it is certainly the exception.

These "expert" books are typically complicated, difficult to read, and woefully short on solutions. I waded through stacks of books bursting with information about human sleep, but all lacked specific solutions to the sleeping-through-the-night-without-crying-it-out dilemma. Sure, the reader learns the mechanics, but still she's left wondering one basic question. *How does she teach her baby to sleep?*

I've presented the information you need in a friendly, easy-to-follow format so that even in your sleep-desperate state, you can find your solutions easily and quickly.

To show you how things were going for me when I began working on the concepts herein, this was Coleton's actual night-waking schedule, logged on tiny bits of paper one very sleepless night.

Coleton's Night Wakings

Twelve months old

8:45 P.M. Lie in bed and nurse, still awake

9:00 Up again to read with David and Vanessa

9:20 To bed, lie down, and nurse to sleep

9:40 Finally! Asleep

11:00 Nurse for 10 minutes

12:46 Nurse for 5 minutes

1:55 Nurse for 10 minutes

3:38 Change diaper, nurse for 25 minutes

4:50 Nurse for 10 minutes

5:27 Nurse for 15 minutes

6:31 Nurse for 15 minutes

7:02 Nurse for 20 minutes

7:48 Up. Nurse, then up for the day

Number of night wakings: 8

Longest sleep stretch: 1½ hours

Total hours of nighttime sleep: 8¼ hours

Naps: One restless nap for ¾ hour

Total hours of sleep: 9 hours

And I did *this* for twelve months! So, you see? If you are there now, you really do have my heartfelt sympathy, because I have been there too. And I can get you out of that sleepless place, just as I did for my baby and myself. That's a promise.

Picking my way though ideas and options, experimenting and applying what I had learned, this is the improvement I experienced after twenty days creating and using my sleep solutions:

Coleton's Night Wakings

Sleep plan in effect: 20 days

8:00 P.M. To bed. Lie down and nurse to sleep

11:38 Nurse for 10 minutes

4:35 Nurse for 10 minutes

7:15 Nurse for 20 minutes

8:10 Nurse. Up for the day

Number of night wakings: 3

Longest sleep stretch: 5 hours

Total hours of nighttime sleep: 11½ hours

Naps: One peaceful nap, one hour long

Total hours of sleep: 12½

Amount of crying involved: ZERO

Success, Day by Day

As my research continued, so did our improvement. In the insightful words of Iyanla Vanzant in her book, *Yesterday, I Cried* (Simon & Schuster, 2000), "All teachers must learn. All healers must be healed, and your teaching, healing work does not stop while your learning, healing process continues."

As Coleton began to sleep better, I was deeply involved in the research and writing of this book, so naturally, I continued to apply what I was learning. More time passed, and Coleton *finally* followed in his sister's footsteps and began sleeping ten hours straight without a peep. (At first, I would wake up every few hours worried. I'd place my hands on his little body to feel for breathing. Eventually I realized he was just peacefully, quietly sleeping.)

This is Coleton's log after using the strategies I'd learned during the writing of this book:

Coleton's Night Wakings

7:50 P.M. Coleton lays his head on my lap and *asks* to go "night night."

8:00 To bed. Lie down to nurse

8:18 Asleep

6:13 A.M. Nurse for 20 minutes

7:38 Up for the day

Number of night wakings: 1 (Improved from 8)

Longest sleep stretch: 10 hours (Improved from 1½)

Total hours of nighttime sleep: 11 hours (improved from 8¼)

Naps: One peaceful nap, two hours long (improved from ¾ hour)

Total hours of sleep: 13 hours (improved from 9 hours)

Amount of crying involved: ZERO

Keep in mind that, during this time, I was actively researching and experimenting with ideas. You have the benefit of following a very tidy plan, so you should have quicker success. Also, certainly, Coleton was different from his sister Vanessa, who at an extremely young age, dove for her crib and woke happily ten hours later. Babies are as different from each other as we adults who raise them. But compare this log to where we started. Even though it took some time to get us to this point, I was ecstatic over our results.

Here's a footnote that will please many of you. Throughout this entire process, Coleton continued to breastfeed and sleep with me. Through my own experience and working with other mothers, I realized that co-sleeping–breastfeeding babies *can* sleep all night next to Mommy without waking to nurse, contrary to popular thinking. If you are determined to continue breastfeeding and co-sleeping, you might be able to do so *and* get some sleep, too!

Use This Book However It Is Helpful to You

The good news is that you, my reader and new friend, need be involved in this process only to the extent that it is helpful to you. I will ask you to do nothing that is uncomfortable for you or anything but gentle for your baby. Use only those ideas that appeal to you; even using a few of them can help you and your baby sleep better.

My goal is to help you *and* your baby sleep all night—without *either* of you crying along the way.

My Test Mommies

Once I had found success with Coleton, I searched out other families who were struggling with their baby's night wakings. I gathered a group of sixty women who were enthusiastic about trying my sleep ideas. This test group is a varied and interesting bunch! When we first met, their babies ranged in age from two months to twenty-seven months. One even had a five-year-old with sleep problems. For some, this is a first baby, some have older siblings, and one mother has twins. Some of the mothers work outside the home; some work only at home. Some bottle-feed, some breastfeed. Some co-sleep, some put their babies to sleep in a crib, and some do a little of both. Some are married, and some are single. My test mommies live all across the United States and Canada, with a few from other countries as well. They are all very different from one another—yet they are all exactly the

same in one important way: when we first met they were all struggling with sleepless nights.

These mothers dutifully completed sleep logs every ten days
and E-mailed me on a regular basis to keep me informed of their
progress. They asked questions (boy, did they ask questions!), and
as we worked through my sleep plan, they provided the information and feedback that helped me refine my ideas.

Proof! It Works!

At the start of our work together, *none* of the sixty mothers had
babies who were sleeping through the night, according to the
medical definition of the phrase, which is when a baby sleeps for
a stretch of five or more hours without waking.

As the test mommies followed ideas in *The No-Cry Sleep
Solution*:

- By day ten, 42 percent of the babies were sleeping through
  the night.
- By day twenty, 53 percent were sleeping through the night.
- By day sixty, 92 percent were sleeping through the night.

Once these babies reached the five-hour milestone, they continued on with more sleep success, some achieving sleep stretches
of nine to thirteen hours.

How Long Will It Take for Your Baby to Sleep?

Please keep in mind that making this transformation takes time.
No crying, but no rushing either. I wish you *could* have results in

one day—I certainly can't promise that—but I can promise that things *will* improve as you follow the suggestions.

The irrefutable truth is that we cannot change a comfortable, loving-to-sleep (but waking-up-all-night) history to a go-to-sleep-and-stay-asleep-on-your-own routine without one of two things: crying or time. Personally, I choose time. And this means *patience* and might just represent your first opportunity to teach that particular virtue to your child.

Parents have asked for my help because their *five-year-old* is still waking up at night. Take heart, and keep things in perspective. My new sleep plan will *not* take five years to produce the desired effect!

The Test Mommies' Experiences

It really does help to know what other parents have experienced. The following is what a few of the test mommies had to say.

Lisa, a mother of two girls, ages one and five—both with sleep problems—said in her first letter to me:

> I co-slept with Jen, our five-year-old, until she was about a year old, at which time we tried to move her to her own bed. Since that time, she comes into our room EVERY night. Yes, every night for the past four years! Our baby Elizabeth . . . well, at age one she is still getting up three to five times a night. I feel extreme anxiety. During the night, I hear the minutes ticking away on the clock that sits on my nightstand, waiting for one or the other to call for me, and with each minute everything seems to intensify. I often just break down and cry. As I sit here this morning with my coffee next to me, things don't seem quite SO bleak, but I have to admit that I still feel like crying. I just can't do this anymore. HELP.

Five weeks later I received this E-mail from her:

I know it's not time for another log for us, but I just had to tell you what's been going on. Beth has been going to sleep at 8:30 and waking only ONCE! And getting up at 7:30! I can't believe it!

Jennifer has also been in HER OWN ROOM *ALL* night for ten days in a row now! She's so proud of herself, and I am so proud of her too!

IT'S WORKING! IT'S WORKING! IT'S WORKING!

Kim, the single mother of thirteen-month-old Mathieau had this to say when we first started to work on her baby's sleep habits:

Well, things aren't going according to my plan at all. I tried to get him down at 7:30—I tried rocking him, nursing him, putting him in his crib, patting his back, rocking again, and nursing again, and he finally gave out at 8:45. I honestly don't know what the problem was tonight. I just hope it won't continue to be like this. I want so badly for this to work, I'm very frustrated.

Three weeks later, Kim had this to say:

Hi! I know I E-mailed you a couple of days ago about Mathieau sleeping through the night, but I just had to share this with you. Mathieau has slept through the night three—yes, count them, three—nights in a row. Can you believe it? I actually feel like a functional mommy now. He let me sleep in this morning too. He woke around 6:30 this morning to nurse and went back to sleep until 9. I had so much energy today. And even more, the baby-sitter has finally been able to get him to nap, too! Today when I picked him up he was still asleep—he had been sleeping for almost two hours! I am so excited that your ideas are actually working for us. I never expected to see this kind of result so quickly. We have made some MAJOR progress, and we couldn't have done it without your ideas. You are definitely on to something here and you are going to be changing many people's lives.

The mother of a three-month-old, Christine expressed these feelings when we first spoke:

> Ryan's night wakings are becoming very stressful on our family. My husband can no longer sleep in bed with us, so he has grudgingly moved to the guest room. I am petrified I won't be able to function when I go back to work if I am going to continue to be up with him all night like this. I tried to let him cry it out, but it was a nightmare to see my normally happy, peaceful little baby crying so hard and sweating and looking so afraid and alone. I really hope you can help us.

Her log, just forty-five days later, says it all.

7:30 P.M. Asleep
6:00 A.M. Feed
7:30 A.M. Up for the day
Number of night wakings: 1 (improved from 10)
Longest sleep stretch: 10½ blissful, wonderful hours (improved from 3)
Total hours of nighttime sleep: 10½

Emily, mother of twelve-month-old Alex, included this information in her first message to me:

> Alex sleeps with his mouth on my breast and his body horizontally across mine. He sometimes will sleep next to me, but only until he wakes up again, which is sometimes only five minutes later, and then it is back on top of me.

Alex's triumphant mother sent me this message after thirty days following the No-Cry Sleep Solution:

This will be my final log now that my little Alex is sleeping wonderfully. He is asleep by 8:00 P.M., and then I set him in our bed while I usually get up and shower or clean up. (Of course, we have mesh guardrails and we watch him carefully.) Alex may wake up once during the night to nurse, but it only takes him seconds to fall back asleep. I think he may wake up several other times during the night, but he doesn't need my assistance to go back to sleep. He wakes around 7:30 A.M. feeling happy and refreshed.

I can't believe this is the same baby as before. The difference in his sleep habits is truly amazing.

And this from Marsha, another mother of a chest-sleeping baby:

Last night Kailee went to bed at 8:30. She woke up a few times between 8 and 10 but quickly settled herself. I didn't hear from her again until 8:00 A.M.! I am sure you understand that this is complete and total heaven. Kailee has gone from needing to sleep on my chest all night and waking up to nurse eight to ten times a night to sleeping 11–12½ hours straight through. I never thought I would see the day when a baby of mine would sleep through the night. You are a hero in our house. I definitely wish you had been doing this study when my first daughter was a baby.

And remember the mother I quoted earlier who said, "I am truly distressed, as the lack of sleep is starting to affect all aspects of my life"? Two months after Leesa started following my plan, she wrote, "For the last week Kyra has been waking only ONCE, at 3:30 A.M., to nurse! Heeeheeeheeee! I'm darn near giddy on sleep!"

More quotes from the test mommies appear throughout this book in sections called Mother-Speak. Pictures of their sweet, sleeping babies are also sprinkled throughout this book.

You Can Sleep, Too

There are no good reasons for you to live as a sleep-deprived martyr. There *are* ways to get your baby to sleep without resorting to all-night cryathons. Action is key—action that will strengthen you and motivate you as you move through these next few weeks. So give the No-Cry Sleep Solution a try and plan on seeing results. You may not go straight from waking up every hour to sleeping ten consecutive hours, but you *will* go from waking every hour to every three . . . to every four hours . . . to, eventually, that all-night milestone, and more.

Shortly after which *you* will resume waking every hour, waiting for the car to pull into the driveway, keys to plop on the kitchen table, and footsteps to resound on the stairs up to your teenager's room. It really does go so fast.

Please be *patient* as you move through the steps. This is so very important. When your baby is unhappy or starts to cry (I said "starts" to cry, not wails for ten minutes!), go ahead and pick him up, rock him, nurse him, or whatever your heart tells you to do to soothe your sweet baby. Every day will move you one step closer to your goal, and knowing that, you can be more loving and patient.

Remember, too, that your baby's apparent inability to fall asleep on her own is not her fault. She's done things this way

Mother-Speak

"I understand that it will take a while to see positive results. But after seven months of total sleep deprivation and exhaustion, just knowing that I'll be sleeping in another month or so seems like salvation."

Tammy, mother of seven-month-old Brooklyn

since the day she was born, and she'd be perfectly happy to keep things as they are. The goal is to help her feel loved and secure while you help her find ways to fall asleep without you.

In summary, I don't believe a baby should be left alone to cry himself to sleep. Or even left to cry as you pop in every ten minutes to murmur comforting words without reaching out to touch him. But I also know that you can—gently and lovingly—help your baby to sleep *peacefully* all night long.

Part I

Ten Steps to Helping Your Baby Sleep All Night

This section of the book will cover the steps to follow as you create your own sleep solution. You may want to use this page as a checklist as you go through the steps:

☐ Step One: Do a Safety Check (page 27)

☐ Step Two: Learn Basic Sleep Facts (page 41)

☐ Step Three: Create Your Sleep Logs (page 53)

☐ Step Four: Review and Choose Sleep Solutions (Newborns—page 64; Babies from Four Months—page 89)

☐ Step Five: Create Your Personal Sleep Plan (page 159)

☐ Step Six: Follow Your Plan for Ten Days (page 169)

☐ Step Seven: Do a Ten-Day Log (page 173)

☐ Step Eight: Analyze Your Success (page 177) and revise your plan as necessary

☐ Step Nine: Follow Your Plan for Ten More Days (page 205)

☐ Step Ten: Complete a Log, Analyze Your Success, and Revise Your Plan as Necessary Every Ten Days (page 215)

1

Do a Safety Check

Because you haven't had quality sleep since before pregnancy or since your new baby entered your life, you may feel that nothing is more important right now than getting a full night's sleep. But there is indeed something much more important than sleep: your baby's safety. So it's critical that we start there.

In their quest for a few more minutes of shut-eye, well-intentioned, but sleep-deprived parents make mistakes. I have heard and read about many situations in which parents put their babies in unsafe situations, all in the name of a few hours of sleep. Here are a few of those stories. I've listed only those with happy endings—but sadly, many other stories end differently.

- Parents of a newborn knew they shouldn't have their fluffy quilt in bed with the baby, but they were cold without it. One night, the mother woke to find that her baby had burrowed under the heavy quilt.
- One baby's mother was so elated when her baby fell asleep on the sofa that she left him there to nap while she went to work at her computer. A loud thump had her running to the family room where she found her baby crying on the floor.
- A mother with a baby who refused to nap admitted that when her baby fell asleep in the car seat, she left her to sleep in the garage while she went in to make dinner. She didn't want to risk waking her up by moving her to her crib.

- Parents of a baby boy received a beautiful antique crib with an ornate headboard from relatives. They'd intended to investigate the safety features of the crib but hadn't gotten around to it. One night, their screaming baby woke them. They ran quickly to his room and found him wedged between the headboard and the mattress.

Many of the safety mistakes that parents make are because of poor decisions, while others are because of a lack of knowledge. You need to know a lot when it comes to your baby's safety. In this important chapter, you'll learn the need-to-know things about your baby's sleep-related safety.

Safety First

Yes, you're tired, too tired perhaps to read through the vast body of information, research, and guidelines out there on the subject of safety. Maybe you'll get to it soon, but your good intentions are not enough to keep your baby safe, and you need this information right now.

No matter how tired you are, no matter how tempting the situation seems, please be sure that you put your baby's safety above all else.

I've gathered safety information from a wide variety of reputable sources and authorities, including the Consumer Product Safety Commission (CPSC), the American Academy of Pediatrics (AAP), the Sudden Infant Death Syndrome Alliance, the National Institute of Child Health and Human Development, and the Foundation for the Study of Infant Deaths. And from all this, I have created sleeping-safety checklists for your review. Please read this brief section, and give it serious consideration.

Keep in mind that these lists cover safety issues relating to *sleep* at *home*. You should, of course, be aware of many other safety issues—at home and away. Also, because safety precautions are updated constantly—and because all babies (and their families) are different—no checklist is fully complete and appropriate for every child. I ask that you please talk with your pediatrician about your particular baby. Do your homework, and please, put safety first.

The Foremost Safety Worry: SIDS

Sudden Infant Death Syndrome (SIDS) is one of the main safety concerns of all parents of babies. SIDS is the sudden and unexplained death of an infant younger than one year old. SIDS, sometimes known as crib death, is a major cause of death in babies from one month to one year of age. Most SIDS deaths occur when a baby is between one and four months old. The death is sudden and unpredictable; in most cases, the baby seems healthy. Death occurs quickly, usually during sleep. After thirty years of research, scientists still cannot find a definite cause or set of causes for SIDS or a way to predict or prevent it. But research has uncovered some factors that appear to reduce the risk, which I have incorporated into the safety information and lists that follow. (This information about SIDS is from the U.S. Public Health Service, American Academy of Pediatrics, SIDS Alliance, and Association of SIDS and Infant Mortality Programs, SIDS "Back to Sleep" Campaign.)

Back to Sleep

Many babies may sleep better and longer on their tummies. However, a number of studies have scientifically proved that babies who sleep on their tummies are more susceptible to SIDS. This is a statistical percentage meaning that not every baby who sleeps on her tummy will die of SIDS, and avoiding tummy sleeping is

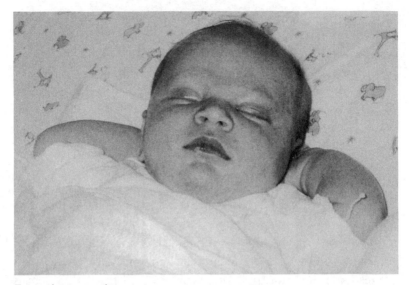

Zoey, three weeks

not a 100 percent guarantee against it. Nevertheless, it is the most important recommendation for you to know about. While a few babies actually benefit from tummy sleeping, back sleeping is safest for most. You'll need to talk with your pediatrician about your particular baby.

Several theories support the back-to-sleep recommendation. One is that some babies who die of SIDS fall into a deep sleep and do not raise their heads to get oxygen. The other theory is that pressure on a tiny baby's chest compresses his diaphragm, preventing him from taking sufficiently full breaths. Regardless of the reason, the fact remains that, with all of the unknowns surrounding SIDS, putting your baby to sleep on her back is the single action that is proven to decrease risk.

In all of my research, I have been unable to pin down an exact age when belly sleeping is safe. However, most researchers tend to imply that once your baby is holding her head up steadily and rolling from belly to back and back to belly quite easily on her own, you can put her to sleep on her back and then let her find her own comfortable position. In the meantime, once your doctor confirms that back sleeping is best for your baby, please put her to sleep on her back. If you have a little one who resists this sleep position, you can use the following suggestions to encourage back sleeping.

- Let your baby nap in a car seat, stroller, or infant seat. Sleeping in any of these will keep your baby slightly curled, rather than flat on a mattress; many tummy sleepers enjoy that position much better. Just be sure to follow all safety precautions, which includes keeping baby nearby. (Manufacturers of all car seats, strollers, and infant seats warn parents to never to leave a baby alone in any of these seats.) Watch to be sure your baby doesn't curl too far forward.
- If your baby is a newborn, try swaddling her for sleep. (See page 83.) Being wrapped in a blanket prevents her natural startle reflexes from waking her up.
- Wait until your baby is in deep sleep before gently turning him over. You will recognize this stage by his limp limbs and even, steady breathing.
- Talk to your doctor about the possibility of a compromise: side sleeping. Ask if a sleeping wedge or tightly rolled baby blanket can be used to hold your baby in this position.
- Although various products are available to keep a baby in the back-sleeping position, their safety has not been tested, and at this time they are not recommended. At this writing, several sleep wraps have been designed to hold a baby swaddled in a back-sleeping position and they are just becoming available. Ask your doctor or hospital about any new inventions.
- Finally, if you still choose to have your baby sleep on her tummy, or if your doctor has approved this position, make

certain that the mattress is even, firm, and flat, and that every time you put her to bed, the sheets are smooth and tightly secured. Also, don't put any pillows, blankets, or toys in bed with her. If you still have concerns, ask your doctor or hospital about renting a sophisticated baby monitor so that you can keep track of sound, movement, and breathing.

Once your baby is sleeping on her back:

- Don't let her sleep in the exact same position every night and nap. Move her head from one side to the other, and vary her position in the crib, or the placement of the crib itself, to encourage her to look in all directions. This will prevent the back of your baby's head from becoming flat (a condition called positional plagiocephaly).
- Avoid leaving your baby lying on her back in a stroller, car seat, or swing for long periods during the day.
- Place your baby on her tummy often when she is awake to encourage head and body movement and physical development of all muscle groups.

Back Sleeping at Day Care

According to some studies, 20 percent of SIDS deaths occur in child-care settings. Not all child-care centers have policies on infant sleep positions, and even when they do, not all child-care providers abide by the AAP's recommended guidelines. It's important for you to know that babies who are not used to sleeping on their stomachs are at a particularly high risk for SIDS if they are placed in this position for sleep. Check on the policies in your child-care center, and be sure that they are placing your baby in the proper sleep position as recommended by your doctor.

General Sleeping Safety Precautions for All Families

- Do not allow anyone to smoke around your baby. This holds true whether your baby is asleep or awake. Babies who are exposed to smoke face an increased risk of SIDS, as well as other health complications, such as asthma.
- If your child spends time with a child-care provider, baby-sitter, grandparent, or anyone else, insist that safety guidelines are followed in that environment also.
- Keep your baby warm, but not *too* warm. Keep the bedroom at a comfortable sleeping temperature, usually between 65°F and 72°F (18°C to 22°C). Be careful not to overheat your baby. If your newborn comes home from the hospital wearing a hat, ask your doctor if he should wear it to sleep and for how long. A hat could contribute to overheating.
- Do not use blankets or comforters under or over the baby. They can entangle your baby or become a suffocation hazard. Instead, when the temperature warrants, dress your baby in warm sleeper pajamas layered with an undershirt.
- Dress your baby in flame-resistant and snug-fitting sleepwear, not oversized, loose-fitting cotton or cotton-blend clothing. Billowy or cotton fabrics pose a burn hazard in

case of fire or even with a close encounter with your stove or fireplace.

- Do not allow your baby to sleep on a soft sleeping surface such as a pillow, sofa, water bed, beanbag chair, pillow-top mattress, foam pad, sheepskin, feather bed, or any other soft and flexible surface. Baby should sleep only on a firm, flat mattress, with a smooth, wrinkle-free sheet that stays securely fastened around the mattress.
- Do not leave stuffed toys or pillows in bed with your baby. You may leave a small, safe "lovey" as described on pages 117–119 with a baby more than four months old who can roll over and lift and move his head easily.
- Keep night-lights, lamps, and all electrical items away from where Baby sleeps.
- Make sure you have a working smoke detector in Baby's sleeping room, and check it as often as the manufacturer suggests.
- Do not put a baby to sleep near a window, window blinds, cords, or draperies.
- If your baby is sick or feverish, call your doctor or hospital promptly.
- Keep your baby's regular appointments for well-baby checkups.
- Never shake or hit your baby. (The National Commission on Sleep Disorders Research concluded that infant abuse often occurs when a parent is sleep-deprived and at the end of his or her rope. If you feel like you may lose your temper with your baby, put her in a safe place or with another caregiver, and go take a breather.)
- Never tie a pacifier to your baby with a string, ribbon, or cord, as any of these can become wound around your baby's finger, hand, or neck.
- Follow all safety precautions when your baby is sleeping away from home, whether in a car seat, stroller, or unfa-

miliar place. Take extra time and care to create a safe sleep-ing place for your baby, no matter where you are.

- Never leave a baby unattended while in a stroller, baby seat, swing, or car seat.
- Never leave a pet with access to a sleeping baby.
- Learn how to perform infant cardiopulmonary resuscitation (CPR). Be sure that all other caregivers for your baby are also trained in infant CPR.
- Keep your baby's environment clean. Wash bedding often. Wash your hands after diapering your baby and before feed-ing. Wash Baby's hands and face frequently.
- Breastfeed your baby whenever possible. Breast milk decreases the risk of certain illnesses and infections, which, in turn, can decrease the risk of SIDS and other health problems.
- Pay attention to your own health and well-being. If you have feelings of anxiety, panic, confusion, sadness, regret, irritability, or hopelessness, you may be suffering from post-partum depression. Please see your doctor and explain your symptoms. This condition is common, and treatment is available.

General Safety Precautions for Cradles and Cribs

- Make certain your baby's crib meets all federal safety regu-lations, voluntary industry standards, and guidelines of the CPSC's most recent recommendations (cpsc.gov). Look for a safety certification seal. Avoid using an old or used crib or cradle.
- Make sure the mattress fits tightly to the crib or cradle, without gaps on any side. (If you can fit more than two fin-

gers between the mattress and side of the crib or cradle, the mattress does not fit properly.)

- Make certain that your crib sheets fit securely and cannot be pulled loose by your baby, which may create a dangerous tangle of fabric. Do not use plastic mattress covers or any plastic bags near the crib.

- Remove any decorative ribbons, bows, or strings. If you use bumper pads, make certain they surround the entire crib and that they are secured in many places—at a minimum, at each corner and in the middle of each side. Tie securely, and cut off dangling string ties.

- Remove bumper pads before your baby is old enough to get up on his hands and knees. If your baby can pull himself to stand, make sure the mattress is on the lowest possible setting. Also, inspect the area around the crib to make sure no dangers await him if he does climb out of the crib.

- Be certain that all screws, bolts, springs, and other hardware and attachments are tightly secured, and check them from time to time. Replace any broken or missing pieces immediately. (Contact the manufacturer for replacement parts.) Make sure your crib or cradle has a sturdy bottom and wide, stable base so that it does not wobble or tilt when your baby moves around. Check to see that all slats are in place, firm, and stable—and that they are spaced no more than 2⅜ inches (60 millimeters) apart.

- Corner posts should not extend more than ¹⁄₁₆ inch (1½ millimeters) above the top of the end panel. Don't use a crib that has decorative knobs on the corner posts or headboard and footboard designs that present a hazard, such as sharp edges, points, or pieces that can be loosened or removed. Always raise the side rail and lock it into position. Make sure your baby cannot operate the drop-side latches.

- Don't hang objects over a sleeping or unattended baby— that includes mobiles and other crib toys. There is a risk of the toy falling on your baby or of your baby reaching up and pulling the toy down into the crib.

- If you are using a portable crib, make sure the locking devices are properly and securely locked.
- Make sure your baby is within hearing distance of your bed or that you have a reliable baby monitor turned on.
- Check the manufacturer's instructions on suggested size and weight limits for any cradle, bassinet, or crib. If there is no tag on the crib, call or write the manufacturer for this information.
- Any crib or cradle your baby sleeps in when away from home should meet all of the above safety requirements.

General Safety Precautions for Co-Sleeping

The safety of bringing a baby into an adult bed has been the subject of much debate. All four of our babies have been welcomed into our family bed. My husband, Robert, and I have naturally allowed our children to share our bed, and our children have enjoyed sleeping in a sibling bed as well. The fact that we have religiously followed known safety recommendations for sharing sleep with our babies is of the utmost importance.

However, in the interest of keeping you informed and presenting a legal disclaimer, I must tell you that in 1999 the U.S. CPSC announced a recommendation against co-sleeping with a baby younger than age two. Nevertheless, some polls show that like us, nearly 70 percent of parents do share sleep with their baby either part or all night. Most parents who *do* choose to co-sleep are avidly committed to the practice, and they find many benefits to sleeping with their babies.

The CPSC's warning is controversial and has stirred heated debate among parents, doctors, and childhood development experts about the accuracy and appropriateness of the recommendation, and many experts believe that the issue demands more research. In the meantime, it is very important that you investigate all the viewpoints and make the right decision for your family. Even if you decide that you feel uncomfortable sleeping with your infant, you can look forward to sharing sleep with your older baby if that suits your family.

The following safety list and references to co-sleeping are not intended to be construed as permission but are provided as information for those parents who have researched this issue and have made an informed choice to co-sleep with their baby.

Wherever you choose to have your baby sleep, it is important to take safety precautions. If your baby sleeps with you, either for naps or at nighttime, you should adhere to the following safety guidelines:

- Your bed must be absolutely safe for your baby. The best choice is to place the mattress on the floor, making sure there are no crevices that your baby can become wedged in. Make certain your mattress is flat, firm, and smooth. Do not allow your baby to sleep on a soft surface such as a water bed, sofa, pillow-top mattress, or any other flexible surface.
- Make certain that your fitted sheets stay secure and cannot be pulled loose.
- If your bed is raised off the floor, use mesh guardrails to prevent Baby from rolling off the bed, and be especially careful that there is no space between the mattress and headboard or footboard. (Some guardrails designed for older children are not safe for babies because they have spaces that could entrap them.)
- If your bed is placed against a wall or other furniture, check every night to be sure there is no space between the mattress and wall or furniture where Baby could become stuck.
- Infants should be placed between their mother and the wall or guardrail. Fathers, siblings, grandparents, and baby-sitters

don't have the same instinctual awareness of a baby's location as mothers do. Mothers, pay attention to your own sensitivity to Baby. Your little one should be able to awaken you with minimum movement or noise—often even a sniff or snort is enough to wake a baby's mother. If you find that you are such a deep sleeper and you only wake up when your baby lets out a loud cry, you should seriously consider moving Baby out of your bed, perhaps into a cradle or crib near your bedside.

- Use a large mattress to provide ample room for everyone's movement.
- Consider a sidecar arrangement in which Baby's crib or cradle sits directly beside the main bed as one option.
- Make certain that the room your baby sleeps in, and any room he might have access to, is child-safe. (Imagine your baby crawling out of bed to explore the house as you sleep. Even if he has not done this—yet—you can be certain he eventually will!)
- Do not ever sleep with your baby if you have been drinking alcohol, have used any drugs or medications, are an especially sound sleeper, or are suffering from sleep deprivation and find it difficult to awaken.
- Do not sleep with your baby if you are a large person, as a parent's excess weight has been determined to pose a risk to Baby in a co-sleeping situation. While I cannot give you a specific parent's weight to Baby ratio, you can examine how you and Baby settle in next to each other. If Baby rolls toward you, if there is a large dip in the mattress, or if you suspect any other dangerous situations, play it safe and move Baby to a bedside crib or cradle.
- Remove all pillows and blankets during the early months. Use extreme caution when adding pillows or blankets as your baby gets older. Dress Baby and yourself warmly. (A tip for breastfeeding moms: wear an old turtleneck or T-shirt,

cut up the middle to the neckline, as an undershirt for extra warmth.) Keep in mind that body heat will add warmth during the night. Make sure your baby doesn't become overheated.

- Do not wear any night clothes with strings or long ribbons. Don't wear jewelry to bed, and if your hair is long, pin it up.
- Don't use strong-smelling perfumes or lotions that may affect your baby's delicate senses.
- Do not allow pets to sleep in bed with your baby.
- Never leave your baby alone in an adult bed unless it is perfectly safe. For example, placing Baby on a mattress on the floor in a childproof room when you are nearby or listening in with a reliable baby monitor.
- As of the writing of this book, there are no proven safety devices for use in protecting a baby in an adult bed. However, as a result of the great number of parents who wish to sleep safely with their babies, a number of new inventions are beginning to appear in baby catalogs and stores. You may want to look into some of these nests, wedges, and cradles.

2

Learn Basic Sleep Facts

Much of the literature about babies and sleep suggests that a parent read an entire book of facts on human sleep before making any changes. When your eyelids threaten to droop before the first chapter is read, this becomes an exercise in futility. The facts aren't learned, the plan doesn't get made, the problem doesn't get solved, and one more parent is resigned to another year or two or three of sleep deprivation.

So here, I'll try to give you just the information you need, short and concise, with a few basic and important sleep facts that are important to know. This way, you can get on to the real reason you're reading this book: to devise and implement the right sleep plan for you and your baby.

How Do We Sleep?

We fall asleep, we sleep all night, and then we wake up in the morning. Right? Wrong! During the night, we move through a sleep cycle, riding it up and down like a wave. We cycle through light sleep to deep sleep to dreaming all through the night. In between these stages, we briefly come to the surface, without awakening fully. We may fluff a pillow, straighten a blanket, or roll over, but generally we fade right back into sleep with nary a memory of the episode.

Our sleep is regulated by an internal body clock scientists have dubbed the *biological clock* or *circadian rhythm* ("around a day" in Latin). And they have discovered that, strangely, this clock is set on a twenty-five-hour day—meaning we must continuously reset it. We do this mainly with our sleep-wake routines and exposure to light and darkness.

This biological clock also has specific times of day that are primed for sleep or wakefulness. This is the cause of jet lag as well as the sleep problems that plague shift workers. This is also why it's often difficult to awaken on Monday morning—sleeping in and going to bed late during the weekend disrupt established rhythms, and we must reset our internal clocks, starting with the moment the alarm rings on Monday morning.

This circadian rhythm affects how alert we feel during various parts of the day. There are natural times for sleep and for wakefulness. The brain seeks a state of biochemical balance of sleep and wakefulness, and when the scale is heavy toward sleep, we feel tired. This rhythm explains why many people have a midafternoon slump, and why some cultures routinely incorporate a siesta (afternoon nap) into the day. The human biological clock has a natural afternoon drop in alertness, followed by a period of wakeful energy that lasts until later in the evening, when there is an onset of drowsiness. These patterns change as life stages do. A baby's pattern is not the same as an older child's, a child's is different from an adult's, and an adult's is different from an elderly person's.

How Do Babies Sleep?

A baby is not born with an adult circadian rhythm. A newborn baby's sleep-wake cycles are spread throughout day and night,

Gavin, ten months old

gradually settling into a pattern of defined naps and nighttime sleep.

A baby's biological clock begins maturing at about six to nine weeks of age and does not work smoothly until about four to five months. As the biological cycle matures, a baby reaches a point when she is mostly awake during the day and mostly asleep during the night. At about nine to ten months, a baby's sleep periods consolidate so that she wakes up and goes to sleep at about the same times every day, and her sleep spans are longer.

Because the biological clock is the primary regulator of daily sleep and wakefulness patterns, it is easy to see why a baby does not sleep through the night—and why this pattern so adversely affects new parents!

Babies move through the same sleep cycles as adults do, but their cycles are shorter and more numerous. Babies also spend much more time in light sleep than adults do, and they have many more of those in-between stages of brief awakenings. There are two reasons why a baby sleeps like a baby.

The first is developmental. A baby's sleep pattern facilitates brain growth and physical development. Babies grow at an astronomical rate during the first two years of life, and their sleep patterns reflect biological needs that differ vastly from those of adults.

The second reason why a baby sleeps like a baby is survival. They spend much of their time in lighter sleep. This is most likely so that they can easily awaken in uncomfortable or threatening situations: hunger, wetness, discomfort, or pain. In fact, acclaimed pediatrician Dr. William Sears, in *The Baby Book* (Little, Brown and Company, 1993) says, "Encouraging a baby to sleep too deeply, too soon, may not be in the best survival or developmental interests of the baby."

All the stages of sleep are important for your baby's growth and development. As he matures, so does his sleep cycle; attaining sleep maturity is a *biological* process.

A Baby's Sleep Cycle

Understanding that a baby naturally and necessarily follows a particular sleep cycle is crucial to understanding her problems with falling asleep and staying that way. A typical baby's nighttime sleep cycle looks something like this:

Drowsy; falling asleep
Light sleep
Deep sleep for about an hour
Brief awakening
Deep sleep for about one to two hours
Light sleep
Brief awakening

Rapid eye movement (REM); dreaming sleep
Brief awakening
Light sleep
Brief awakening
REM (dreaming sleep)
Brief awakening
Toward morning: another period of deep sleep
Brief awakening
REM (dreaming sleep)
Brief awakening
Light sleep
Awake for the day

The Likely Culprit of Your Sleep Troubles? Those Brief Awakenings!

Now you know that brief awakenings (night wakings) are a normal part of human sleep, regardless of age. All babies experience these. The difference with a baby who requires nighttime care every hour or two is that he is involving the parent in all his brief awakening periods. This conclusion was the lightbulb moment in my own research—and seems so obvious, now that I understand sleep cycles and their physiology.

Typically, when a frequent night-waking baby wakes up and starts to cry, he's not hungry or thirsty or wet or even lonely; he's just plain tired, as desperate for sleep, perhaps, as his parents but, unlike them, clueless as to how to fall back asleep!

Imagine this. *You* fall asleep in your nice, warm, comfy bed with your favorite pillow and your soft blanket. When your first night waking occurs, you may change position, pull the covers up, and then fall right back to sleep without ever remembering this happening.

What if you woke up to find yourself sleeping on the kitchen floor without blankets or a pillow?

Could you simply turn over and go back to sleep? I know *I* couldn't! You would probably wake up startled, worry about how you got there, fret a bit, go back up to bed, get comfortable, and eventually fall asleep—but not too deeply, because you would worry about winding up back on the floor again. This is how it is for a baby who is nursed, rocked, bottlefed, or otherwise parented to sleep. She falls asleep rocking, nursing, sucking a pacifier, and so forth and wakes up to wonder, "What happened? Where am I? Where's Mommy and Daddy? I want things the way they were when I fell asleep! Wahhh!"

Your baby makes a sleep association, in that she associates certain things with falling asleep and believes she *needs* these things to fall asleep. My baby, Coleton, spent much of his first few months in my arms or on my lap, his little head bobbing to the tune of my computer keyboard. From the very moment he was born, he slept beside me, nursing to sleep for every nap and every bedtime. By the time I looked up, he was twelve months old, firmly and totally entrenched in a breastfeeding-to-sleep association.

This sleep association philosophy is explained in nearly every book on babies and sleep. When the association is described, no gentle solutions are ever given. It is with the intent of "breaking" this association that the cry-it-out process is recommended. In my opinion—one you probably share, since you've chosen this book—this is a very harsh and insensitive way to teach a baby a new association, particularly when he's learned to associate sleep with a loving ritual such as breastfeeding or being held and rocked in a parent's arms while enjoying a warm bottle. (And what is the new association? "Crying alone in my crib in the dark is the way I fall asleep"? Not a very pleasant alternative.)

Chapter 4 explains the myriad alternatives to crying it out, ways to slowly and lovingly help your baby create new falling-to-sleep associations. (For the best results from this book, please follow all the steps in order. Learning about these basic facts is an important step. Don't rush ahead just yet.)

What Is a Sleep Problem?

During the first year of life, a baby wakes up frequently during the night. As you have now learned, this is not a problem. It is a biological fact. The *problem* lies in our perceptions of how a baby should sleep and in our own needs for an uninterrupted night's sleep. We parents want and need our long stretches of sleep to function at our best in our busy lives. The idea then is to slowly, respectfully, and carefully change our baby's behavior to match our own needs more closely.

How Much Sleep Do Babies Need?

Table 2.1 on page 48 is only a guide; all babies are different, and some truly do need less (or more) sleep than shown here, but the vast majority of babies have similar sleep needs. If your baby is not getting *close to* the amount of sleep on this chart, he may be chronically overtired—and this will affect the quality and length of both his nap and nighttime sleep. Your baby may not *seem* tired, because overtired babies (and children) don't always *act* tired—at least not in the ways we expect. Instead, they may be clingy, hyperactive, whiny, or fussy. They may also resist sleep, not understanding that sleep is what they really need.

Mother-Speak

"This describes Melissa to a 'T.' When she's overtired she gets really whiny and clingy and she fights sleep like it is the ultimate enemy! Yet, if she doesn't get a nap, she actually ends up sleeping less at night, and having more night wakings."

Becky, mother of thirteen-month-old Melissa

This guide can be very helpful as you analyze your baby's sleep habits.

Table 2.1 Average hours of daytime and nighttime sleep for babies

Age	Number of naps	Total length of naptime hours	Nighttime sleep hours*	Total of nighttime and naptime sleep
Newborn**				
1 month	3	6–7	8½–10	15–16
3 months	3	5–6	10–11	15
6 months	2	3–4	10–11	14–15
9 months	2	2½–4	11–12	14
12 months	1–2	2–3	11½–12	13–14
2 years	1	1–2	11–12	13
3 years	1	1–1½	11	12
4 years	0	0	11½	11½
5 years	0	0	11	11

*These are averages, and they do not represent unbroken stretches of sleep.

**Newborn babies sleep 16–18 hours per day, distributed evenly over six to seven brief sleep periods.

What About Nighttime Feedings?

We have all heard about those three-month-old babies who sleep ten to twelve straight hours every night, without waking to eat. Why these babies sleep so soundly is a mystery. But, when we hear about these amazing babies, we assume *all* babies can and should do this, and we become very discouraged when our five month old, eight month old, or twelve month old is *still* waking up twice a night for feeding.

To my surprise, sleep specialists—even the toughest cry-it-out advocates—agree that up to twelve months of age, *some* children truly *are* hungry after sleeping for about four hours. They recommend that if your child wakes up hungry, you should promptly respond by feeding her.

Mother-Speak

"Sometimes when Carrson would wake up in the night I'd actually hear his tummy growling."

Pia, mother of eight-month-old Carrson

Experts also agree that to grow and thrive, a baby may not only want but may also *need* one or two night feedings up to about nine months of age. Dr. Sears says that even an eighteen-month-old child may need a before-bed feeding to set aside his hunger until morning. Of course, it can be difficult to know if your baby is hungry or just looking to use nursing or a bottle for comfort. As you follow the steps in this book, your baby will begin to wake up less often just for comfort and your company, and it will become more obvious when he is waking up because he is hungry.

Mother-Speak

"When Emily was able to understand my questions I would ask her 'Are you hungry?' If she said yes, I would take her downstairs to the kitchen for a snack. This was short-lived because she learned she'd rather stay in bed."

Christine, mother of eighteen-month-old Emily

As a baby's system matures she will be able to go for longer periods at night without eating. This is a biological process. Up until that time, research shows that feeding a baby solid food at night doesn't help her sleep longer—although some mothers do swear that it makes a difference with their babies. If your doctor gives you the go-ahead to feed your baby solids, you can experiment with this. Don't rush it, though. Babies who start solids too early tend to develop more food allergies, so it's not wise to start too soon.

So it stands to reason that if your baby has slept about four hours, wakes, and appears hungry, you should consider feeding him. (This is especially important if your baby is younger than four months old.) Maybe he will then sleep another four hours instead of waking frequently from hunger! Also, some babies go through growth spurts when they are eating more during the day, and they may eat more at night, too.

What Are Realistic Expectations?

Most babies awaken two to three times a night up to six months, and once or twice a night up to one year; some awaken once a night from one to two years old. A baby is considered to be sleeping through the night when she sleeps five consecutive hours, typically from midnight to 5:00 A.M. While this may not be *your* definition of sleeping through the night, it is the reasonable yard-stick by which we measure Baby's sleep. That's five hours—*not* the eight, ten, or twelve hours we may wish for! The difficult aspect of this is that if you put your baby down to sleep at 7:00 P.M., you probably then go about catching up on your daily tasks. Just about the time you head for bed, your baby has already slept four or five hours and may be ready for your attention.

The good news is that, if your baby is biologically ready, you can encourage progress toward that five-hour milestone; once your baby reaches it, you can take steps to lengthen this night-time stretch. This book will tell you how.

What Is the *Right* Way to Teach a Baby to Sleep?

William C. Dement, M.D., Ph.D., considered the world's leading authority on sleep, sleep deprivation, and sleep disorders, and founder of the world's first sleep disorder center at Stanford University, explains in *The Promise of Sleep* (Dell Trade Paperback, 2000):

> No scientific experiments have been done on how best to train an infant to sleep, but I can make a few conjectures. I doubt that a regular pattern of sleeping and being awake can ever be imposed on infants immediately after birth or that anyone should even try. Their biological clocks seem to need to mature before they can keep track of the time of day. But the same kinds of cues that work for us should work on infants' clocks as they are maturing.
>
> Once you understand how much sleep your child needs, the most important strategy for improving his or her sleep is to set a daily rou-

tine and stick to it. Between the ages of five months and five years, the social cues imposed by parents become the primary factor in children's sleep patterns.

According to Dr. Dement, setting a routine and developing healthy bedtime cues and nighttime associations will allow your baby to drift off to sleep. *The No-Cry Sleep Solution* will help you create such a routine, customized for your baby and your family.

Now that you have learned some important basic sleep facts, you will use this knowledge as a foundation for developing your sleep plan. The first step, as outlined in the next chapter, will be to create sleep logs that will give you a clear picture of how your baby is sleeping now. Once you identify the issues that are preventing your baby from sleeping, we will move along to the solutions for helping your baby sleep—peacefully and happily—without your constant nighttime attention. And *without* "crying it out."

3

Create Your Sleep Logs

Here's where we get to work! The first step to improved sleep is to get an accurate picture of your baby's current sleep pattern. You'll need to pick a day and night to log what is really happening. There are blank forms for your use at the end of this chapter.

This is a very important step and one that you should not skip in your haste to get started on the sleep solutions. Once you determine exactly how your baby is sleeping now, you'll be able to decide which ideas best apply to your situation, and you'll be able to track your success and make adjustments based on the information you'll glean from your logs.

This is really very simple to do.

Let's Get Started!

Begin by choosing a day to do your sleep logs. The first step will be to jot down information about your baby's naps in the nap log. Knowing exactly how long it takes your baby to fall asleep, where and how he falls asleep, and when and how long he naps will all be important information. Since naptime sleep has a great impact on nighttime sleep, this nap data will be very helpful as you determine what changes you'll need to make in your baby's sleep routines. Here was my nap log for Coleton:

Coleton's Nap Log

12 months old

Time baby fell asleep	How baby fell asleep	Where baby fell asleep	Where baby slept	How long?
1:20	Nursed for 40 minutes	In bed with me	In bed alone	48 minutes

You will find a form for your own nap log on page 59.

On the same day that you complete your nap log you will also do your prebedtime routine log. This information will help you see whether your actions in the evening are helpful in settling your baby for bed or whether they are hindering your baby's ability to settle down for a good night's sleep. Beginning about an hour or two before bedtime, write down everything you do in the prebedtime routine log on page 60.

At each step you will note the time, what activities your baby is engaged in, and the levels of three things:

1. Activity: active, moderate, or calm
2. Noise: loud, moderate, or quiet
3. Light: bright, dim, or dark

Your log will help you take a fresh look at your nighttime routine (or lack thereof!). On the following page you'll see my first prebedtime routine log for Coleton. You may find, like I did, that your evenings are not what you would call a calm, quiet, settling routine for your baby! Later in this book we'll work together to create a calming presleep routine for your baby, but for now, just take a look at what's happening in your house.

Here was mine:

Coleton's Prebedtime Routine Log

12 months old

Time	What we did	Activity level	Noise level	Light level
6:40	Home from shopping; unload car	Active	Loud	Bright
7:00	Change into pajamas; nurse	Calm	Quiet	Dim
7:45	Play in Angela's room; listen to her new CD; sort her nail polish collection	Moderate	Loud	Bright
8:00	Play airplane and tickle with Daddy	Exceptionally active!	Very loud	Bright
8:30	Watch David's and Vanessa's play: *Ninja Man and the FBI in the Rooftop Battle*	Active	Exuberantly loud	Bright
8:45	Lie in bed and nurse	Calm	Quiet	Dark
9:00	Up again to read with David and Vanessa	Calm	Moderate	Dim
9:20	Back in bed, lie down, nurse to sleep	Calm	Quiet	Dark
9:40	Asleep			

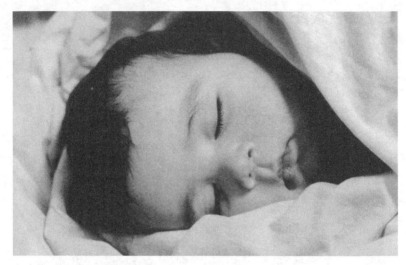

Anjali, nine months old

After you have written down your prebedtime hour, log your baby's awakenings for the night. The easiest way is to put a pile of scrap paper and a pencil next to your bed (not a pen, since in the dark a pencil is more reliable). Place these where you can easily reach them when you wake up during the night. Make sure you can see a clock from where you awaken. Each time your baby wakes up, write down the time. Note how he woke you up (snort, cry, movement). Make a quick note of what you do then—for instance, if you change the baby, write that down. If you are co-sleeping and get out of bed, write that down. If you nurse or give a bottle or pacifier, write that down, too. Make a note of how long your baby is awake, or what time he falls back to sleep. Don't worry about good penmanship or details.

In the morning, immediately transfer your notes to your night-waking log on page 61 (or create one on paper or in your computer) so that they make sense. Do this as soon as possible after waking so that everything is fresh in your mind.

Here was my first log:

Coleton's Night-Waking Log

12 months old

Time	How baby woke me up	How long awake; what we did	Time baby fell back to sleep	How baby fell back to sleep	How long of a sleep stretch since fell asleep*
9:40	Fell asleep nursing				
11:00	Sniff and snort	10 minutes; nursed	11:10	Nursing	9:40–11:00 1½ hours
12:46	Whimper	5 minutes; nursed	12:51	Nursing	11:10–12:46 1½ hours
1:55	Sniff and snort	10 minutes; nursed	2:05	Nursing	12:51–1:55 1 hour
3:38	Whimper (wet diaper)	25 minutes; changed diaper; nursed	4:03	Nursing	2:05–3:38 1½ hours
4:50	Sniff and snort	10 minutes; nursed	5:00	Nursing	4:03–4:50 ¾ hour
5:27	Movement	15 minutes; nursed	5:42	Nursing	5:00–5:27 ½ hour
6:31	Movement	15 minutes; nursed	6:46	Nursing	5:42–6:31 ¾ hour
7:02	Movement, noise making	20 minutes; nursed	7:22	Nursing	6:46–7:02 ¼ hour
7:48	Movement, noise making	Up for the day			7:22–7:48 ½ hour

---

*I chose to round my times to the quarter hour. If you wish, you can use exact times, such as 1 hour 27 minutes. The overall difference is minimal, so you can choose whichever way is most comfortable for you.

At the bottom of your night-waking log you'll find a place to write down a summary of the information in your log. This summary will help you quickly see how your new efforts are affecting your baby's sleep as you try out the ideas presented in this book. This is what my summary looked like:

Asleep time: 9:40 P.M.
Awake time: 7:48 A.M.
Total number of awakenings: 8
Longest sleep span: 1½ hours
Total hours of sleep: 8¼ hours

When you have filled out your three logs, answer the sleep questions that follow the logs. If this is not your own book, you can photocopy the log pages or simply write the information on blank sheets of paper.

When you have completed this groundwork, move on to Chapter 4.

Wonderful ideas, and blissful sleep, lie just ahead. I promise!

Nap Log

Baby's Name: _____

Age: _____

Date: _____

Time baby fell asleep	How baby fell asleep	Where baby fell asleep	Where baby slept	How long?

1. Review Table 2.1 on page 48:
   How many naps *should* your baby be getting? _____
   How many naps is your baby getting *now*? _____
   How many hours *should* your baby be napping? _____
   How many hours is your baby napping *now*? _____
2. Do you have a formal nap routine? _____
3. Are your baby's naptimes/lengths consistent every day? _____

Prebedtime Routine Log

Baby's Name: _____

Age: _____

Date: _____

Key:
Activity: active, moderate, or calm
Noise: loud, moderate, or quiet
Light: bright, dim, or dark

Time	What we did	Activity level	Noise level	Light level

1. Do you have a formal, consistent bedtime routine? _____
2. Is the hour prior to bedtime mostly peaceful, quiet, and dimly lit? _____
3. Does your bedtime routine help both you and your baby relax and get sleepy? _____
4. Any other observations about your current bedtime routine? _____
   _____
   _____

Night-Waking Log

Baby's Name: _____

Age: _____

Date: _____

Time	How baby woke me up	How long awake; what we did	Time baby fell back to sleep	How baby fell back to sleep	How long of a sleep stretch since fell asleep

Asleep time: _____

Awake time: _____

Total number of awakenings: _____

Longest sleep span: _____

Total hours of sleep: _____

Sleep Questions

1. Review Table 2.1 on page 48:
   How many hours of nighttime sleep *should* your baby be getting? _____
   How many hours of nighttime sleep is your baby getting *now*? _____
   How many total hours of nighttime and naptime sleep *should* your baby be getting? _____
   How many total hours of nighttime and naptime sleep is your baby getting *now*? _____
   How do the suggested hours of sleep compare to your baby's actual hours of sleep?
   Gets _____ hours too little sleep
   Gets _____ hours too much sleep
2. Is your baby's bedtime consistent (within ½ hour) every night? _____
3. Do you "help" your baby to go back to sleep every time, or nearly every time he or she awakens? _____
   How do you do this? _____
4. What have you learned about your baby's sleep by doing this log?
   _____
   _____
   _____
   _____

4

Review and Choose
Sleep Solutions

Once you have done a safety check, learned about basic sleep facts, and completed your initial sleep logs, you are ready to proceed. You will create your baby's customized sleep plan based on the ideas in this chapter. I would strongly suggest that you use all of the suggestions that you think make sense for you and your baby. Stick with them long enough for them to have an impact—at least two or three weeks. One or two nights isn't enough to judge an idea's value. This is *not* a quick-fix plan, but it *is* a plan that will work. It *is* a plan that will enable you to help your baby sleep better. You just need to choose your solutions, organize your plan, make a commitment, and stick with it.

The ideas in this section are separated into two parts. The first is especially for newborns, the second part is for babies who are more than four months old. The ideas are clearly described in both sections. In the older babies section, the ideas are coded for five different types of babies to make it easy for you to choose from them.

- Breastfed
- Bottlefed
- Crib sleeper
- Co-sleeper
- Pacifier user

Many of the ideas are good for everyone.

Read through all the ideas and note those you think could help your baby sleep better. Then, just transfer the information to the personal sleep plan, which begins on page 160. This will consolidate all your ideas in one place for easier reference. Prepared with your solutions, you can then begin to follow your personal plan. (Go ahead and start using one or two of the ideas along the way if you'd like. The sooner you get started, the better!)

Part One: Solutions for Newborn Babies— Birth to Four Months

(If your baby is older than four months you can skip to page 89.)

Congratulations on the birth of your new baby. This is a glorious time in your life. Whether this is your first baby or your fifth, you will find this a time of recovery, adjustment, sometimes confusion and frustration, but—most wonderfully—of falling in love.

Newborn babies do not have sleep problems, but their parents do. Newborns sleep when they are tired, and wake when they are ready. If their schedule conflicts with yours, it's not a problem for them; they don't even know it.

Mother-Speak
"The effects of your ideas are less dramatic if you use them from the beginning—but less dramatic is a good thing when it comes to a baby's sleep!"

Judith, mother of three-month-old Harry

You are very lucky to be reading this book *now*. The things that you do during the first few months will set a pattern for the next year or two or more. You can take steps during the next few months that will help your baby sleep better. You can do this in a gentle, loving way that requires no crying, stress, and rigid rules. Applying some general ideas over the next few months can set the stage for better sleep for the years to follow.

I advise you to read through the section on older babies that follows this one, because you will learn a lot from those ideas; do keep in mind, however, that babies younger than four months old have very different needs than older babies. This section about newborns will help you understand your baby's developing sleep patterns as they are *now*.

When your baby reaches four months of age, you can begin using those ideas for older babies. However, if you read, understand, and apply the following tips for newborns while your baby is still indeed a newborn, you may not need this book when your baby is four months old. Isn't that a wonderful thought?

Mother-Speak

"Based on my friends' experiences, I was expecting a year of sleepless nights ahead of me. I am so happy that my baby is already sleeping six straight hours! My friends call it a miracle!"

Yelena, mother of seven-month-old Samantha

Read, Learn, and Beware of Bad Advice

Absolutely *everyone* has an opinion about how you should raise your baby. Remembering back to when my first child was born, I was amazed at how many people felt compelled to share their advice. One day, when Angela was just a few days old, a friend—

a single, male, childless friend, I must add—came by to visit and see the new baby. She was napping at the time, and we were chatting. Angela awoke with a cry, and I popped up to get her. He laughed and said, "Oh, you don't have to *run* to her. When babies cry, they don't even know where the sound is coming from!" (Where, I wondered, did he learn *that* bit of nonsense?)

The danger to a new parent is that these tidbits of misguided advice (no matter how well-intentioned) can truly have a negative impact on our parenting skills and, by extension, our babies' development, if we are not aware of the facts. The more knowledge you have the less likely that other people will make you doubt your parenting skills.

My mission, and that of the other esteemed and informed parent educators who share the bookshelves with me, is to present the facts as we know them, so you can *choose* your approach from the proactive strength of knowledge and not the reactive weakness of ignorance. In other words, if you inform yourself, then you protect yourself and your family from the barrage of "shoulds" and "woulds" that don't fit you or your family and that may even have no evidence or supporting facts.

That's the game plan that the interesting conversation with my single, male, childless friend prompted me to develop. I realized that, had I not been informed and confident on this particular issue, my friend's opinion would have left me confused, worried, and self-doubting. At the very least, he did manage to shock me speechless.

So, your best defense is knowledge. It really is power, as they say. It's the light that illuminates the dark halls (or cribs, in this case) of ignorance. The more you know, the more easily you will develop your own philosophies about child rearing. When you have your facts straight, and when you have a parenting plan, you will be able to respond with confidence to those who are well-meaning but offering contrary or incorrect advice.

So, your first step is to get smart! Know *what* you are doing, and know *why* you are doing it. Then, when those amateur experts share their advice, you can smile, say "Oh, really?" and then go about your business, with quiet confidence, in your own way.

There are a number of outstanding books about babies in the marketplace. I suggest that you read a baby book or two and build your store of knowledge. Your books will probably be well-used, highlighted, and dog-eared because you'll find yourself referring to them often in the first few years of your baby's life. Choose your books wisely; ask for recommendations from friends who share your parenting beliefs, and find authors who have philosophies that match your own way of thinking. As you read, keep in mind that no author will parallel your beliefs 100 percent, so you must learn to take from each one the ideas that work best for your family. Here are a few of my favorites:

The Baby Book, William Sears, M.D. and Martha Sears, R.N. (Little, Brown and Company, 1993)
Attachment Parenting, Katie Allison Granju and Betsy Kennedy (Pocket Books, 1999)
Your Baby and Child: From Birth to Age Five, Penelope Leach (Knopf, 1997)
What to Expect the First Year, Arlene Eisenberg, et al. (Workman Publishing, 1996)

In my book, I will help you learn about babies and sleep. The best place to start, of course, is at the beginning.

The Biology of Newborn Sleep
During the first several months of your baby's life, he simply sleeps when he's tired. His waking-sleeping pattern mainly revolves around his stomach. He's awake when he's hungry and asleep when he's full. You can do very little to force a new baby

to sleep when he doesn't want to, and conversely, you can do little to wake him up when he is sleeping soundly.

A very important point to understand about newborn babies is that they have very, very tiny tummies. New babies grow rapidly, their diet is liquid, and they digest it quickly. Formula digests quickly, and breast milk digests even more rapidly. Although it would be nice to lay your little bundle down at a predetermined bedtime and not hear a peep from him until morning, even the most naïve among us know that this is not a realistic goal for a tiny baby. Newborns need to be fed every two to four hours—and sometimes more. During those early months, your baby will have tremendous growth spurts that affect not only daytime but nighttime feeding as well, sometimes pushing that two- to four-hour schedule to one to two hours around the clock.

Mother-Speak

"I remember when Rachel was a newborn, she would suck away happily for most of the day for a week or two at a time. Had I not known that this sometimes happens, and that it is necessary for the wild growth babies sometimes experience, I might have tried to enforce a schedule. Instead, I simply accepted my role in life then: a binky with legs."

Vanessa, mother of two-year-old Rachel

Babies are unpredictable, and a handful of them will make their own rules. Some newborns will sleep four or five hours straight, leaving their parents to worry if they should wake them for a feeding. The answer to this is an unequivocal "maybe." If your baby happens to fall into this pattern you'll need to talk to your doctor and find out if it's OK for your particular baby to stretch time between feedings. This will depend on your baby's size, health, and possibly other factors as well.

Sleeping Through the Night

You have probably read or heard that babies start "sleeping through the night" at about two to four months of age. What you must understand is that, for a new baby, a five-hour stretch (the one I mentioned earlier) *is* a full night. Many (but nowhere near all) babies at this age can sleep uninterrupted from midnight to 5 A.M. (Not that they always do.) A far cry from what you may have thought sleeping through the night meant!

Here we pause while the shock sinks in for those of you who have a baby who sleeps through the night but didn't know it.

If your baby is already sleeping through the night, enjoy the heady privilege of bragging rights next time the old childbirth education group meets. But, if you're thinking of putting this book away now, not so fast. Babies are fickle, and "it ain't over 'til it's over."

Mother-Speak

"By two months old our little Emily was sleeping a seven-hour stretch every night. But instead of developing that into a longer night's sleep, she went in reverse, until she was waking every three to four hours. Luckily, your sleep solutions have helped us fix that!"

Christine, mother of eighteen-month-old Emily

What's more, while the scientific definition is five hours, most of us wouldn't consider that anywhere near a full night's sleep. Also, some of these sleep-through-the-nighters will suddenly begin waking more frequently, and it's often a full year or even two until your little one will settle into a mature, all-night, every-night sleep pattern. This book is full of ideas that will help you work *with* your baby to encourage that pattern sooner than later.

Where Baby Wants to Sleep

Where does your baby feel the most comfortable and secure? *In your arms.* Where is your baby most at peace? *In your arms.* If given the choice, where would your new baby tell you she *wants* to sleep? *In your arms,* of course!

There is nothing—absolutely nothing—as endearing and wonderful as a newborn baby falling asleep in your arms or at your breast. I know that I found it nearly impossible to put my sleeping Coleton down. Maybe because having this fourth baby at age forty-one, I knew he was my last baby and that he would grow up all too soon. Or, maybe not, given that I also did this with my first baby, Angela, fourteen years ago. Come to think of it, I did it with Vanessa and David, too. So, maybe, just maybe, it's something else. Maybe the "mother lion" instinct takes over when I have a new baby. Maybe it's because mothers are biologically programmed to crave their babies in their arms. And maybe I felt this urge because my reading and my curiosity opened me to it, and blocked out the clutter that today's rush-rush lifestyle imposes.

Whatever the reason, I can tell you that I became an expert at typing with one hand. I can do—and have done—anything with a sleeping baby in my arms—including coaching my daughter's softball team (dugout baby in team-colored sling), chairing a PTA meeting, and even using the toilet. (Oh, you thought you were the only one to do that?)

But—Danger! Alert! Warning! A baby who always sleeps in your arms will—you guessed it—always want to sleep in your arms. Smart baby! A baby who cries for the comfort of her mother's or father's arms, and the parent who responds, is working within the natural framework of instinct that has helped ensure infants' survival from the beginning of time.

This very natural and all-consuming connection would work perfectly in a perfect world—where mothers do nothing but care for their babies that entire first year or two of life. A world in which someone else tends the home, makes the meals, provides the means to pay the bills—while Mommy and baby spend their days enjoying each other and doing those nourishing, bonding things nature intended. Alas, such a world no longer exists, if it ever did. Contemporary life, with its demands, does not provide such privilege. We mothers have much to do, and we must strike a balance between instinct and practicality.

A Forward-Thinking Suggestion

So, as difficult as it may be, I hope you will learn from my mistake. When your baby is asleep, *put him down in his bed.* Don't deprive yourself completely of the precious pleasure of infant sleep, though. Do enjoy this treat once in a while. But unless you think you can spend hours each day with a two-year-old on your lap, it's better that you let him get used to sleeping in his bed.

For those of you who choose to co-sleep with your baby, the idea to sometimes put your baby down alone for sleep is *extremely* important. Babies need much more sleep than adults do. I've worked with many mothers whose babies are so used to Mom's presence in bed that Mom has to put *herself* to bed at 7:00 and *stay there* because her baby has built-in radar that won't allow her to leave him alone. Mommy also has to take daytime naps, whether she wants to or not! The idea is to enjoy the co-sleeping times with your baby, but teach him that he *can* sleep by himself, too.

Good Advice, Briefly Modified

After I wrote the above section, I took a break to pick up my teenaged daughter from an early-release day at school. We spent the afternoon together—had manicures and then went out for lunch. As we sat and talked and giggled like girlfriends, I thought how terribly I would miss her when, in a few short years, she'll leave the nest for college or wherever her nearly adult status takes her. When Angela and I returned home from our outing, the two of us sat with baby Coleton while he entertained us by making faces and noises. His new level of maturity has brought him to the point where he knows when he's funny, and so he purposely exaggerates those things that make others laugh.

I am now thinking that every *moment* of our children's lives is incredibly precious and irreplaceable. How fleeting each phase, and how I wish I could bottle and save each of them to view and treasure. So my advice to put your baby down to sleep is so easily passed out from where I sit. I'll be totally honest with myself and with you, though. If I were to have a fifth child, I'm certain that the new baby would find him- or herself exactly where the others did—sleeping in my arms—with his or her little head bopping to the tune of my computer keys.

So, allow me to amend my advice just a bit, please. Understand that those beautiful, bonding, peaceful habits are very hard to

---

Mother-Speak

"You know, when Zach fell asleep nursing in my arms, I did just this. I traced the outline of his nose, I smelled his hair. I played with his fingers. I wanted to suck up every little thing I could about him when he was a baby, because he is my fourth child, and I'd learned how very quickly it all goes."

Vanessa, mother of two-year-old Zachary

break, so choose them carefully. If you can, and when you can, put your baby down so that she learns she is able to sleep alone, as well as in your arms. And when you don't put her down, hold her with your heart, too, and relish every gurgle, flutter, and little sighing breath. Trust me when I say, "You will miss this." You *will*. Even the dark, exhausted nights will take on a certain romance in your memories, and they'll bubble to the surface when your "baby" drives off in his first car, graduates from school, gets married, has his *own* baby.

Falling Asleep at the Breast or Bottle

It is very natural for a newborn to fall asleep while sucking at the breast, on a bottle, or with a pacifier. As a matter of fact, some newborn babies do this so naturally, and so often, that mothers become concerned that they never eat enough.

When a baby *always* falls asleep this way, he learns to associate sucking with falling asleep; over time, he cannot fall asleep any other way. A large percentage of parents who are struggling with older babies who cannot fall or stay asleep are fighting this natural and powerful sucking-to-sleep association.

Therefore, if you want your baby to be able to fall asleep without your help, it is essential that you sometimes let your newborn baby suck until she is sleepy, but not totally asleep. As often as you can, remove the breast, bottle, or pacifier and let her finish falling asleep without something in her mouth. When you do this, your baby may resist, root, and fuss to regain the nipple. It's perfectly OK to give her back the breast, bottle, or pacifier and start over a few minutes later. Repeat. Repeat. Repeat. If you do this often enough, she will eventually learn how to fall asleep without sucking.

Please go back and reread the previous paragraph. It contains possibly the most important idea I can share with you at this time

Anjali, two months old, and Tina

to assure that you won't be rereading this book eighteen months from now.

The next step in this plan is to try putting your baby in his bed when he is *sleepy* instead of *sleeping*. A tired newborn, too young yet to have ingrained habits, will often accept being put into his crib or cradle while still awake, where he will then fall asleep on his own. When you try implementing this idea, sometimes your baby will go to sleep, and sometimes he won't. When your baby *doesn't* settle and fusses instead, you can rock, pat, or even pick him up and give him back the breast, bottle, or pacifier and start over either in a few minutes or for his next nap.

So you see, over the first few months of life, you can gradually and lovingly help your baby learn how to fall asleep without your help. And you can do this without tears (yours or his).

What About Thumb and Finger Sucking?

If your baby falls asleep sucking her fingers, this is an entirely different situation from using a bottle, pacifier, or the breast. If your baby has to find comfort in sucking her fingers, she is learning to control her own hands and will not always depend on someone else to help her. Current philosophies disagree as to whether letting a baby get into this habit is a good idea, but most experts agree that letting a young baby suck her own fingers poses no harm. The biggest problem, as you may expect, is that some babies don't give up the habit at any age, and you eventually have to step in.

Waking for Night Feedings

Many pediatricians recommend that parents shouldn't let a newborn sleep longer than three or four hours without feeding, and the vast majority of babies wake far more frequently than that. (Remember, too, that there are a few exceptional babies who can go longer.) No matter what, your baby *will* wake up during the night. (See Chapter 2.) The key is to learn when you should pick her up for a night feeding and when you can let her go back to sleep on her own.

This is a time when you need to really focus your instincts and intuition. This is when you should try very hard to learn how to read your baby's signals.

Here's a tip that I am amazed to have never read in a baby book, but is critically important for you to know. Babies make many sleeping sounds, from grunts to whimpers to outright cries, and these noises don't always signal awakening. These are what I call sleeping noises, and your baby is nearly or even totally asleep during these episodes. These are not the cries that mean, "Mommy, I need you!" They are just sleeping sounds. I remember when my first baby, Angela, was a newborn sleeping in a cradle next to my bed. Her cry awakened me many times, yet she was asleep in my arms before I even made it from cradle to rocking chair to sit down. She was making sleeping noises. In my desire to respond to my baby's every cry, I actually taught her to wake up more often!

You need to listen and watch your baby carefully. Learn to differentiate between sleeping sounds and awake and hungry sounds. If she is really awake and hungry, you'll want to feed her as quickly as possible. If you do respond immediately when she is hungry, she will most likely go back to sleep quickly. But, if you let her cry escalate, she will wake herself up totally, and it will be harder and take longer for her to go back to sleep. Not to mention that *you* will then be wide awake, too!

> Listen carefully when your baby makes night noises:
> If she is making sleeping noises—let her sleep.
> If she really is waking up—tend to her quickly.

For Breastfeeding or Co-Sleeping Mothers

As I was researching this book, it became obvious to me that a great many new mothers spend part or all of their nights sleeping with their babies. (If you are part of this group, please review the section on safe co-sleeping starting on page 37.) When you breastfeed and co-sleep with your baby, your sleep cycles will probably become synchronized. This means that you will both experience midcycle awakenings at the same time. When this happens, it is a beautiful sign that you and your baby have found perfect sleep harmony; and it will make your night waking easier, because when your baby wakes you won't be roused from a state of deep sleep. It is easy for you, in your partially awake state, to attach your baby to your breast, and then, when your baby easily falls back to sleep, so do you.

Dr. James J. McKenna, director of the Mother Baby Behavioral Sleep Center at the University of Notre Dame, in an article for The Natural Child Project website says:

> My colleagues and I observed mother-infant pairs as they slept both apart and together over three consecutive nights. Using a polygraph, we recorded the mother's and infant's heart rates, brain waves (EEGs), breathing, body temperature, and episodes of nursing. Infrared video photography simultaneously monitored their behavior.
>
> We found that bed-sharing infants face their mothers for most of the night, and that mother and infant are highly responsive to each other's movements, wake more frequently, and spend more time in lighter stages of sleep than they do while sleeping alone. Bed-sharing infants nurse almost twice as often, and three times as long per bout, as they do when sleeping alone. But they rarely cry. Mothers who routinely sleep with their infants get at least as much sleep as mothers who sleep without them.

During the night, when both you and your baby are in your brief awakening periods, he may simply breathe noisily or move around, and you'll automatically attach him to the breast; the two of you will both drift back off to sleep. This is a wonderful, peaceful experience when you have a newborn lying beside you, and can be a new mother's best solution for much-craved sleep.

But beneath the surface of this peaceful scenario lies a problem. Your baby will come to expect a nursing at every brief awakening. And if you recall from Chapter 2, which described basic sleep facts, (you *did* read that, right?) your baby has a brief awakening every hour or so all night long. While you may find this arrangement acceptable for the early newborn months, it's a very rare mother who will still be enjoying it ten or twelve months later.

Sleeping Noises
The key is to get your co-sleeping baby to feel comfortable sleeping next to you without having to order from Mommy's all-night snack bar every hour! The important concept for obtaining this balance is described in the section called Waking for Night Feedings on pages 75–76. As I describe there, babies make a wide assortment of sleeping noises. Not all of these mean, "I'm awake and want to nurse." A co-sleeping mother's best long-term sleep enhancer is to learn how to pretend to be asleep while listening to Baby's sounds. And to wait. Your baby just may fall back to sleep without your help. If she needs to breastfeed, you'll know that soon enough.

Help Your Baby Distinguish Day from Night

A newborn baby sleeps about sixteen to eighteen hours per day and this sleep is distributed evenly over six to seven brief sleep periods. You can help your baby distinguish between nighttime and daytime sleep, and thus help him sleep longer periods at night.

Begin by having your baby take his daytime naps in a lit room where he can hear the noises of the day, perhaps a bassinet or cradle located in the main area of your home. Make nighttime sleep dark and quiet. This means no talking, singing, or lights in the middle of the night. If your home is noisy after baby's bed-time, use white noise to cover up the sounds of the family. White noise can be soft background music, the hum of a heater or fan (safety precautions taken), or any other steady sound. You can even purchase small clock radios with white-noise functions (they sound like spring rain or a babbling brook), or cassette tapes with quiet nature sounds or even sounds from the womb.

You can also help your baby differentiate day naps from night sleep by using a nightly bath and a change into pajamas to sig-nal the difference between the two.

Keep your nighttime feedings quiet and mellow. There's no need to talk or sing to your little one in the middle of the night; save all that for daytime.

Nighttime Bottle-Feeding with Ease
If you are bottle-feeding your baby, make sure that everything you need for night feeding is close at hand and ready to use. Your goal is for baby to stay in a sleepy stage and nod right back off to sleep. If you have to run to the kitchen to prepare a bottle, while baby fusses or cries, you'll just bring both of you to the point of being wide awake, and what may have been a brief night waking will turn into a long period of wakefulness.

Nighttime Diapers
If your baby is waking every hour or two during the night, you don't have to change her diaper every time. Again, remembering back to when Angela was a newborn and I was a "newmom," I dutifully changed her every hour or two when she woke up. Oftentimes I was changing one dry diaper for a new one. I even-tually learned that I was more "tuned in" to the diaper issue than she was!

I suggest that you put your baby in a good-quality nighttime diaper, and when she wakes, do a quick check. Change her only if you have to, and do it as quickly and quietly as you can in the dark. Use a tiny night-light when you change the baby, and avoid any bright lights that can signal daytime. Have your changing supplies organized and close to Baby's bed, and make sure you use a warm cloth to wipe that sleepy bottom. (Check into the many available types of baby-wipe warmers, and keep one near your nighttime changing station.)

Nighttime Cues
You will want to create special cues that signal bedtime sleep. A consistent, exact bedtime routine that begins at least thirty minutes before sleep time is very helpful in getting baby to organize his day/night sleep pattern. (You can read more about bedtime routines on pages 100–103.)

Don't Let Baby Nap Too Long

Try not to let your newborn take too long of a nap. If your little one is sleeping a lot during the day, including a three- to five-hour stretch, and then getting up frequently at night, she may have her days and nights mixed up. (Of course, there are those few babies who take long naps and then sleep well at night, but if your baby were like this you wouldn't be reading this book now, would you?)

Not allowing too long of a nap is sometimes a hard rule to keep. When you are sleep deprived, and you have gotten behind on your own chores and responsibilities, it's easy to "take advantage" of your baby's long nap to catch up. While this may be helpful in the short run, it can interfere with nighttime sleep, which makes it harder for you to function during the day. It also delays the time when your baby organizes her sleep into short, daytime naps and long, nighttime sleeps.

This is one of the times when we can break that rule of never waking a sleeping baby. If your baby has napped more than two or three hours, wake her gently, and encourage her to stay awake for a while and play.

Some babies, like my second child, Vanessa, are such sleepy newborns that an earthquake can't wake them! We have a family portrait with a sleeping four-week-old Vanessa in her Daddy's arms because absolutely nothing would wake her for the picture. Here are a few tips for waking such a sleepy baby when it's time to get up and eat:

- Try to wake your baby during a lighter stage of sleep. Watch for movement in arms, legs, and face. If your baby's limbs are dangling limply, she'll be especially hard to waken.
- Give Baby a diaper change or wipe his face with a damp washcloth.
- Unwrap your baby and undress her down to her diaper and T-shirt (in a warm room).
- Burp him in a sitting position.
- Give Baby a back rub.
- Take off her socks and rub Baby's feet or wiggle her toes. Play "this little piggy."
- Move Baby's arms and legs in a gentle exercise pattern.
- Prop Baby in an infant seat in the middle of the family's activity.
- Hold your baby upright and sing to her.

You might also be able to shorten these excessive naps by putting him down for his nap in a room with daylight and some noise, and keeping nighttime sleep very dark and quiet.

Newborn babies do sleep a lot during the day. But this will change very soon. It can be a challenge to learn how to go about your usual daily routines with a baby along, but it's important that you begin to see your baby as a little person who keeps you company throughout the day. Don't feel that you must save every task for the times when your baby is sleeping. Begin now to include your awake baby in your everyday chores. After all, babies love to watch and learn, and you are your baby's most important teacher. She will enjoy becoming a part of your daily life, and you will enjoy her company, too.

Watch for Signs of Tiredness

One way to encourage good sleep is to get familiar with your baby's sleepy signals, and put her down to sleep as soon as she seems tired. A baby cannot put herself to sleep, nor can she understand her own sleepy signs. Yet a baby who is encouraged to stay awake when her body is craving sleep is typically unhappy. Over time, this pattern develops into sleep deprivation, which further complicates your baby's developing sleep maturity.

Mother-Speak

"I discovered that I had been putting Carrson to bed by the clock, not by his tiredness. Once I changed this dynamic he fell asleep easier and slept longer."

Pia, mother of eight-month-old Carrson

Most newborns can only handle about two hours of wakefulness. Once Baby becomes overtired, he will become overstimulated and find it harder to fall asleep and stay asleep. Look for that magic moment when Baby is tired, but not overtired. These are some of the signs your baby may show you—he may demonstrate only one or two; you'll get to know your baby over time:

- A lull in movement and activity
- Quieting down
- Losing interest in people and toys (looking away)
- Looking "glazed"
- Fussing
- Rubbing eyes
- Yawning

Learn to read your baby's sleepy signs and put him to bed when that window of opportunity presents itself.

Make Your Baby Comfortable

Babies are as different from each other as we adults are, and you'll learn to understand your own baby over time. Here are a few ideas for making babies comfortable. Experiment with them, and you'll soon discover which are best for your little one:

Swaddling

Babies arrive fresh from an environment (the womb) in which they were held tightly. Some babies are most comforted when parents create a womblike setting for sleep by wrapping them securely in a receiving blanket. Your pediatrician, a veteran parent, or a baby book can give you step-by-step instructions for swaddling your baby. If your baby enjoys swaddling, you might want to use it only at night to encourage her to sleep longer. Also, ask your doctor whether *your* baby is safe swaddled in a blanket. Once Baby begins to move about, this *isn't* a safe way for her to sleep, because she can loosen the blanket and become tangled. Another caution: don't swaddle a baby if the room is warm; it can create overheating, which is one of the risk factors of SIDS.

Cozy Cradle

Many new babies simply get lost in a big crib. Your baby may find a smaller cradle or bassinet more to her liking. Many babies even scoot up to the corner of the cradle to wedge their head into the crevice—much like they were wedged into your pelvis. Make sure that if your cradle can rock that you lock it into a stationary position when your baby is sleeping, and that it cannot be tipped over as she does this creeping-into-the-corner routine.

Create a Nest

Because they spent nine months curled into a tight ball, some new babies are not comfortable lying flat on their backs on a firm mattress. However, back sleeping on a firm mattress is the most important protection against SIDS. An alternative that seems to keep many babies happy, and sleeping longer, is to put them to sleep in a car seat, infant seat, or stroller, keeping them in a somewhat curled position. This might help those babies who only sleep well while cradled in Mommy's or Daddy's arms, or snugly curled into a sling. It gives you a gentle method to teach Baby how to sleep out of your arms. Safety rules do require that you keep your baby within eyesight if using this suggestion. In addition, if your baby sleeps in a car seat or baby seat, make sure he doesn't slump over with his head down. This can lead to breathing problems. Help your baby keep his head up by using specially made car-seat padding that provides additional support.

A potential drawback to this idea is that your baby may get used to sleeping in an upright position, which could cause problems later on when he tries to sleep lying down. So intersperse car-seat naps with sleeping on a flat surface.

Soft Sounds

A number of companies now produce heartbeat recordings that duplicate what your baby heard in the womb. These sounds can be comforting to a new baby. As mentioned earlier, quiet music or white noise can work well also.

Good Smells

A baby's sense of smell is more defined than that of an adult. Research shows that a baby can recognize his own mother by her smell. If you have a small, safe stuffed animal or baby blanket, you can tuck it in your shirt for a few hours, and then place it in the cradle while baby sleeps, following all safety precautions.

A Warm Bed

When a sleepy baby is placed on cold sheets, she can be jarred awake. While you are feeding your baby, you can warm her sleeping spot with a wrapped hot water bottle or a heating pad set on low. Remove the warmer from the crib before you lay your baby down, and always run your arm over the entire area to make sure it's not too hot. Another alternative is to use flannel crib sheets rather than the colder cotton ones.

Make Yourself Comfortable

I've yet to hear a parent tell me that she or he loves getting up throughout the night to tend to a baby's needs. As much as we adore our little bundles, it's tough when you're woken up over and over again, night after night. Because it's a fact that your baby *will* be waking you up, you may as well make yourself as comfortable as possible.

Accept Night Wakings with Your Newborn

The first step is to learn to relax about night wakings right now. Being stressed or frustrated about having to get up won't change a thing. This is a lot like a fourth stage of labor—a very, very short period of time in your life, and later on, you probably will not be able to clearly recall the overwhelming fatigue. The situation will improve day by day; and before you know it, your little newborn won't be so little anymore—she'll be walking and talking and getting into everything in sight during the day and sleeping peacefully all night. But you're in this newborn–no-sleep stage now, so do what you can to get through it as comfortably as possible. Here are a few ideas to make your night activities less disruptive for yourself:

- Make your nighttime-feeding place as cozy and comfortable as you can. If you feed your baby while sitting in a chair, I suggest you move your most comfortable chair into Baby's room for now. If you use a rocking chair, make sure it has soft padding on the seat and back. Get yourself a soft footstool, and put a table beside you for your glass of water, a book, a night-light, and anything else that helps these nighttime episodes seem more inviting.

- If you bottle-feed, make sure everything you need is ready and waiting. (Wonderful portable bottle stations are available. Check out the Dusk to Dawn Bottle Warmer at onestepahead.com as one option that I've been told is convenient.)

- Invest in a specially designed nursing pillow or experiment with how to use bed and sofa pillows to support both the baby and you during your feeding sessions.

- If you breastfeed in bed, make sure you are very comfortable. Many mothers complain of a sore back from nursing in bed. This is usually from arching your back to bring breast to baby. Instead, get yourself in a relaxed and restful position and let your baby fold *himself* around *you*. Babies are remarkably flexible and will tuck into whatever space you allow. Even a big eighteen-month-old can get himself comfortably curled into the space provided when you lie on your side and bring your knees up (speaking from lots of experience.)

- If you and your baby co-sleep, make sure the bed is big enough for everyone to get comfortable. If you're squashed, invest in a bigger or second mattress.
- Arrange your schedule around your baby as much as possible during these early months. Avoid planning evening activities that interfere with your bedtime routine or keep you out too late. The world *will* wait for a few months.
- Relax and slow down. This is a very brief time in your life. Put off doing all those less important things in favor of the most important: taking care of your new baby. It's OK— really.

Fill Baby's Tummy Before Sleep

Try to make the last feeding before bedtime a complete one. If baby nods off after feeding from one breast or after taking half a bottle, shift her around, untuck the blanket, tickle those toes, and encourage her to finish the feeding; otherwise, she may wake up very soon to "finish" her feeding.

Create Restful Feeding Sessions

One piece of advice you will hear over and over is "sleep while baby sleeps during the day." Nice idea, but as a busy mom, the last thing I can do is sleep when baby sleeps! And I'm willing to bet your days are just as full as mine. So, long, blissful naps are usually out of the question. But, during the day, you can *rest* while you feed your baby. Your baby will feed frequently during these first few months. It is your *job* to relax and feed your baby. Don't sit there and fret about all those things that you *should* be doing. *This* is what you *should* be doing during these first few months of your baby's life.

Follow these steps each time you sit to feed your new baby:

- Relax.
- Breathe slowly.
- Push your shoulders down, and relax them. (Mothers tend to raise their shoulders during feeding, especially during the first few months. When your shoulders are up around your ears somewhere, this creates muscle tension in your arms, shoulders, and neck.)
- Circle your head to work out the stress.
- Enjoy a few minutes of peaceful baby time; take advantage of this opportunity to gaze at your precious little one. Start making memories.
- Read, if you enjoy it. (Or read to your baby.)
- Watch television or a movie, or listen to music, if any of those things relax you.

Simplify Your Life

Simplify your life as much as you can during these early months of your baby's life. Relax your housekeeping standards. Graciously accept any help that anyone offers to you. (Repeat after me: "Yes, thank you, that would be nice.") Your first priority right now is to take care of your new baby. Martha Stewart will understand.

Have Realistic Expectations

Your newborn baby will not sleep through the night. There are no magic answers and no shortcuts to sleep maturity. If you focus on your wish for a full night's sleep, you'll just push yourself to the point of weeping over what you cannot have right now. The best advice I can give you is to remind yourself that these early months with your baby will pass quickly. And then you'll be looking back fondly on those memories of holding your newborn in your arms.

> I'm a lactation consultant, and I've been working with a mother of a newborn. Today I went over to see her. She was very pleased because he had "slept through the night." I was alarmed because the baby is only five days old, much too young to be sleeping all night without breastfeeding. I asked for details and this is what I discovered. The baby is sleeping with the mother and last night every time he stirred, Mom put him to her breast. The baby suckled a while and went back to sleep quickly and easily. That was what the mother referred to as "sleeping through the night." Isn't that a lovely way for a new mother to think?

Part Two: Solutions for Older Babies— Four Months to Two Years

The following section presents an assortment of ideas geared to babies who are past the newborn stage, up to two years old and sometimes a little older. If your baby is on the young side of this range, you may want to also read the section particularly for newborn babies that begins on page 64.

Get Yourself Ready

This idea may help everyone.
In the course of my research and in my own experience, I have discovered that our own emotions often hold us back from making changes in our babies' sleeping habits. You yourself may be

the very obstacle preventing you from changing a routine that disrupts your life—in this case, your baby's sleep habits. After all, you probably wouldn't be reading this book unless you find your baby's sleep routine difficult to mesh with your own life. So let's figure out if anything is standing in your way.

Examine Your Own Needs and Goals

Before you read another page of this book, you must ask yourself a few questions, and make a decision. In your heart of hearts, are your baby's wakeful ways and your coping strategies truly upsetting to *you*? Or does the problem lie more in the perceptions of those around you? Let me put it another way. Your baby's sleep habits are only problematic if *you* feel they are. Today's society leads us to believe that "normal babies" sleep through the night from about two months on; my research indicates that this is more the exception than the rule. I've discovered that until about age three, a great percentage of children wake up during the night needing a parent's attention. The number of families in your boat could fill a fleet of cruise ships, so don't feel that you must pressure yourself or your baby to fit into some imagined sleeping requirement.

Mother-Speak

"At our last day-care parent meeting, one father brought up the fact that his two-year-old daughter wasn't yet sleeping through the night. This started a lengthy discussion, and I discovered that out of twenty-four toddlers, only six stayed asleep all night long. Since my daughter is waking up several times throughout the night I found it incredibly reassuring that this appeared to be normal toddler behavior."

Robin, mother of thirteen-month-old Alicia

You must figure out where your problem lies. Is it in your baby's routine, in your management of it, or simply in the minds of others? If you can honestly say you want to change your baby's sleep habits because they are truly and personally disruptive to you and your family, then you're ready to read on. But if you feel coerced into changing Baby's patterns because Aunt Martha, Great-Grandma Beulah, your friend from playgroup, or even your pediatrician says that's the way it should be, it's time for a long, hard think.

Every baby is unique, every mother is unique, and every family is unique. Only you can determine the right answers for your situation.

Once you decide how you truly feel about your baby's sleep habits, you can read this book with a better understanding of what you expect from the things that you learn.

This is a good time to take stock. Compare your baby's sleep pattern to the information in Chapter 2, which explains a baby's average sleep requirement. It also covers how often *typical* babies wake up at night. Use that information to help you determine your goals for your baby's sleep.

Certainly, if your little one is waking you up every hour or two (as my Coleton did), you don't have to think long on the question, "Is this disruptive to me?" It obviously is. However, if your baby is waking up only once or twice a night, it's important that you determine exactly how much this pattern is disturbing to you, and decide on a realistic goal. If you are wishing for twelve hours of solid sleep—from 7 P.M. to 7 A.M.—your goal may not be reasonable. After all, waking up once or twice a night is really normal during the first two years of life, even though many books and articles paint a different picture. I have found it odd that when more than 50 percent of babies younger than two years of age wake up during the night this is labeled a "disorder." With that high of a percentage I'd label it "normal." Just because it's

normal, though, doesn't mean you can, or should, live with it.
You can do many things to encourage your baby to sleep longer.

So, be realistic in determining your goal and honest in assessing the situation's effect on your life. Some people can handle
two night wakings easily, while others find that the effect of even
one night waking is just too much to handle. The key is to evaluate whether your baby's sleep schedule is a problem in your eyes
or just in those of the people around you who are not as informed
as you are now about normal sleep patterns.

If your baby's sleep pattern is a problem for you, this book will
help you solve it. And even if you've decided that one or two
night wakings really aren't so bad after all, you can still use these
concepts to gradually help your baby eliminate them sooner than
he would if you didn't change anything at all.

Begin today by contemplating these questions:

- Am I content with the way things are, or am I becoming
  resentful, angry, or frustrated?
- Is my baby's nighttime routine negatively affecting my marriage, job, or relationships with my other children?
- Is my baby happy, healthy, and seemingly well rested?
- Am I happy, healthy, and well rested?
- Based on the facts in this book (see Chapter 2), what is a
  reasonable expectation for my baby at his or her age?
- What naptime and bedtime situation would I consider
  "acceptable"?
- What naptime and bedtime situation would I consider
  "pure bliss"?

Once you answer these questions, you will have a better understanding of not only what is happening with regard to your baby's
sleep, but also how motivated you are to make a change.

Your motivation is a key component to finding success using
this plan.

Reluctance to Let Go of Those Nighttime Moments

A good, long, honest look into your heart may truly surprise you. You may find you actually *relish* those quiet night wakings when no one else is around. I remember in the middle of one night, I lay nursing Coleton by the light of the moon. My husband, the other three kids, and Grandma were all asleep. The house was perfectly, peacefully quiet. As I gently stroked his downy hair and soft baby skin, I marveled at this tiny being beside me—and the thought hit me, "I love this! I love these silent moments that we share in the night. And I love being needed by this precious baby." It was then that I realized I needed to *want* to make a change in our night-waking habits before I would see any sleep success.

You may need to take a look at your own feelings. And if you find you're truly ready to make a change, you'll need to give yourself permission to let go of this stage of your baby's life and move on to a different phase in your relationship. There will be lots of time to hug, cuddle, and love your little one, but if this plan is to

Mother-Speak

"Well, if I'm honest with myself, I must say that I—in no uncertain terms—fit into this category very nicely. I always loved waking with my babies to nurse at night. Snuggling and nursing a soft warm bundle in the semidarkness when the rest of the household is quiet is one of the most wonderful things about being a mommy. We mommies are paid not with a check, but in hugs, cuddles, and kisses. These nighttimes together are the equivalent of making overtime money or maybe a holiday bonus. Is it any wonder I've been reluctant to give that up?"

Donna, mother of nine-month-old Zachary

work, you must truly feel ready to move those moments out of your sleeping time and into the light of day.

Worry About Your Baby's Safety

We parents worry about our babies, and we should! With every night waking, as we have been tending to our child's nightly needs, we have also been reassured that our baby is doing fine—every hour or two all night long. We get used to these checks; they provide continual reassurance of Baby's safety.

As soon as you decide to help your baby sleep for longer time periods, you will probably move into an overprotective "mother bear" response. When three, four, or more hours have passed, you may worry. Is she breathing? Hot? Cold? Wet? Tangled in her sheet? Lying on her tummy?

Mother-Speak

"The first time my baby slept five straight hours, I woke up in a cold sweat. I nearly fell out of bed and ran down the hall. I was so sure that something was horribly wrong. I nearly wept when I found her sleeping peacefully."

Azza, mother of seven-month-old Laila

These are very normal worries, rooted in your natural instincts to protect your baby. Therefore, for you to allow your baby to sleep for longer stretches, you'll need to find ways to feel confident that your baby is safe—all night long.

The best way to do this is to review Chapter 1 and take all necessary safety precautions. You may want to keep your bedroom doors open or your baby monitor turned on so that you know you'll hear her during the night if she needs you.

Co-sleeping parents are not exempt from these fears. Even if you are sleeping right next to your baby, you'll find that you have become used to checking on her frequently through the night. Even when she's sleeping longer stretches, *you* aren't sleeping, because you're still on security duty.

Once you reassure yourself that your baby is safe while you sleep, you'll have taken that first step toward helping her sleep all night.

Belief That Things Will Change on Their Own

You may hope, pray, and wish that one fine night, your baby will magically begin to sleep through the night. Maybe you're crossing your fingers that he'll just "outgrow" this stage, and you won't have to do anything different at all. It's a very rare night-waking baby who suddenly decides to sleep through the night all on his own. Granted, this may happen to you—but your baby may be two, three, or four years old when it does! Decide now whether you have the patience to wait that long, or if you are ready to move the process along.

Too Fatigued to Work Toward Change

Change requires effort, and effort requires energy. In an exhausted state, we may find it easier just to keep things as they are rather than try something different. In other words, when Baby wakes for the fifth time that night, and I'm desperate for sleep, it's so much easier just to resort to the easiest way to get him back to sleep (rock, nurse, or replace the pacifier) than it is to try something different.

Only a parent who is truly sleep deprived can understand what I'm saying here. Others may be able to calmly advise, "Well if things aren't working for you, just change what you're doing." However, every night waking puts you in that foggy state where the only thing you crave is going back to sleep—plans and ideas seem like too much effort.

If you are to help your baby sleep all night, you *will* have to force yourself to follow your plan, even in the middle of the night, even if it's the tenth time your baby has called out for you. The best defense here is to tell yourself, "In a month or two my baby will be sleeping all night long. I can do this for a few short weeks." And you can. (Especially when you consider the alternative: dealing with night wakings for another year or more!)

So, if after reading this section you're sure you and your baby are ready, it's time for you to make a commitment to change. Now. *Tonight.* This is the time.

Get Your Baby Ready

☆ *This idea may help everyone.*

Before you attempt to make any changes in your baby's sleep routine, make certain that she is comfortable, healthy, and well fed. A baby who is hungry, cold, or has an ear infection, allergies, or any other health problem may wake at night because of pain or discomfort. Rule out these issues before you embark on your plan for better sleep. (For more information on medical and health reasons that keep your baby up at night, please see Chapter 8.)

Fill That Daytime Tummy

Make sure your baby is getting enough to eat during the day, especially if he is exclusively breastfed or formula fed. Some babies get in the habit of nursing or drinking bottles all through the night, taking in an inordinate percentage of their daily calories then. To sleep longer at night, these babies need to tip the feeding scales back toward daytime.

For those little ones eating solids, make sure that *most* food choices are healthful ones. Sure, your toddler loves cheese and that's the only thing she'll eat, but the rules of good nutrition say she should be eating more variety. Good nutrition is important for overall health, including good sleep.

Take a look at what your toddler eats in the hours before bedtime. Does he munch on foods that are conducive to good sleep? Some foods are more easily digested than others and are less apt to disrupt sleep cycles. Think "comfort food"—complex, healthful carbohydrates and nourishing proteins. The choices are endless: whole-grain cereals (easy on the sugar!), oatmeal, brown rice, yogurt, cheese, leftover meats. Fruits and frozen peas (for older children who won't choke on them) satisfy sweet cravings.

In contrast, many foods tend to "rev" the body a bit. Look for hidden caffeine and other stimulating substances. While current scientific thought says sugar does not cause hyperactive behavior in children, I still suspect some effect on the ability and willingness to calm down and fall asleep. Sugar cookies and chocolate cake simply aren't good choices for late in the day.

If your toddler, like most, goes on food jags, take heart. Remember that pediatricians look at a child's diet from the stand-

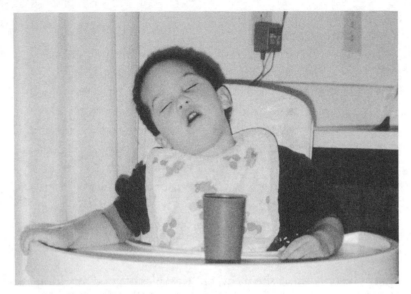

Jarell, twelve months old

point of a week, rather than a day. In other words, when evaluating the healthfulness of your child's diet, think about proportions of major food groups consumed over the course of an entire week.

Breastfeed More During the Day

If your baby is used to frequent night feedings, she is taking in a good portion of her nourishment during those long, relaxed feeding sessions. You may have to nurse more often during the day for a while to make up for the nighttime feedings she will be giving up.

Your baby may be hanging on to night wakings as much for the comfort and emotional connection as for the milk—particularly if you're busy working or tending to other children during the day. If you are sensitive to this, you can give your little one extra cuddles and extra nursings during the day to help her adjust to giving up those nighttime nursing sessions.

Pay attention to the types of foods that *you* eat, because they can affect your breast milk. Watch for your baby's reaction when you drink coffee, tea, or cola, or when you have dairy, nuts, or gassy foods such as broccoli, beans, and cauliflower.

As in the case of little Austen, your curious, busy toddler may be too active to stop during the day to eat or even to nurse. In this case, try providing your energetic baby with "food on the run"—finger food she can carry with her. Another option is to offer her bites of food as she plays. The key is to help her get her full day's calories into the daytime and out of the nighttime.

Mother-Speak

"Austen hardly eats at all during the day and then nurses all night long. I try to offer her food several times a day, but most times she's too busy or distracted to eat. She really likes the time we spend before bed. It seems to always take more than an hour to get her to sleep, and her middle-of-the-night-feeding sessions are long ones."

Annette, mother of twelve-month-old Austen

Check Baby's Nighttime Comfort

Make sure Baby's bed is very comfortable (not *too* soft or yielding as discussed in Chapter 1). Dress him according to the temperature of the room, taking care that he is neither too cold nor too hot. If your home is cool at night, buy thick blanket sleeper pajamas or baby-bag sleepers, and put them on over a T-shirt (the full-body kind that snap at the crotch.) If the season is hot, cool the room with an open window or fan, but follow all the safety rules if you do either of these.

Develop a Bedtime Routine

This idea may help everyone.

A bedtime routine becomes your baby's signal that bedtime is here. It invokes a conditioned response from baby: "Oh! It's bedtime! I should be sleepy!"

A routine for the hour before bedtime is crucial in cueing and preparing your baby for sleep. Include any of the following that you enjoy and that help soothe and quiet your baby:

- Giving Baby a warm, calm bath
- Massaging
- Reading books
- Singing songs
- Playing soft music
- Taking a walk
- Rocking
- Breastfeeding
- Bottle-feeding

The hour before bed should be peaceful. Your routine should be done in rooms with dim lights. Your last step should end in the quiet, dark bedroom with little talking and your usual go-to-sleep technique. Write down your routine, and make it very specific.

A sample bedtime routine would look like this:

1. 7:00 P.M.—Bath
2. Massage with baby lotion
3. Put on pajamas
4. Read three books
5. Lights out
6. Sing lullaby
7. Breastfeed or bottle-feed
8. Rub back
9. Sleep

Use the form on page 162 to write down your own bedtime routine.

Mother-Speak

"We have followed our bedtime routine every night, and I can see that she now expects bed to come after her bath. It's almost like she looks forward to it."

Tammy, mother of seven-month-old Brooklyn

Follow your *exact* routine every night. (Once you and your baby are both comfortable with the routine, and Baby's sleep is consistent, you won't need your written list. This is just to help you establish your routine.) Try to avoid going out at Baby's bedtime during this adjustment period. If you have to go out and come home later than your usual bedtime routine starting point, go through the entire routine, even if you have to shorten the steps—for example, reading just one book instead of three.

A Routine Helps Set Baby's Biological Clock

In addition to the routine itself, if you can put your baby down for naps and bed at about the same time every day, you will achieve sleep success much sooner, because the consistency will help set your baby's internal clock.

An added bonus of this idea is that a specific routine organizes your life, reducing your stress and tension.

A Flexible Routine Is Best

When I talk about "routine" I certainly don't mean a rigid routine that is set in stone! Remember that I'm a mother too, and I know that flexibility is very important when it comes to—oops! I'll be right back. Coleton just woke from a nap and I need to go nurse him, change his diaper, play a little peek-a-boo—I'm back, and as I was saying . . . what was I saying? Oh yes.

Flexibility is important when you have a baby in your life! Try to maintain your bedtime routine as often as possible, but watch your baby too. If your little one is fussing and yawning it's not the time to have a bath and read a bedtime story! It's the time to skip some steps and get him to bed ASAP! You may also have to forfeit your entire routine some nights; if Great-Grandma is having her 100th birthday party don't feel that you have to leave at 6:00 P.M. sharp to get your bedtime routine going. There are times when you'll have to go with the flow and get back to routine the next night.

Bedtime Routine Is Important Throughout Childhood

Don't consider your bedtime routine burdensome, unimportant, or unnecessary. A loving bedtime routine is *always* important for children. Until about age ten or so, a child thrives on spending special quiet time with a parent before bed. Reading books, talking, giving back rubs, and simply being together quietly are all important prebed rituals. Actually, I find that most parents who do *not* have a formal bedtime routine typically spend that last hour before bed fighting with their children about going to bed—now *that* is unpleasant and unnecessary.

At some point, a child no longer needs the ritual, and most parents mourn that loss. My own bedtime routine with my oldest, Angela, has changed over the years. We used to spend that hour cuddling in bed and reading together. Now it begins when I peek my head in her bedroom door. She puts her telephone aside, gives me a kiss and hug, and tells *me* to sleep well. I then climb into my bed while she resumes her homework conference call. Life changes, and so do those bedtime routines.

Establish an Early Bedtime

⭐ **This idea may help everyone.**

Many people put their babies to bed much too late, often hoping that if baby is "really tired" he will sleep better. This often backfires because baby becomes overtired and chronically sleep-deprived. In *The Promise of Sleep* (Dell, 2000), Dr. William C. Dement (the leading authority on sleep whom I mentioned earlier) states, "The effects of delaying bedtime by even half an hour can be subtle and pernicious [very destructive]" when it comes to babies and young children.

A baby's biological clock is preset for an early bedtime. When parents work with that time, a baby falls asleep more easily and stays asleep more peacefully. Most babies are primed to go to sleep for the night as early as 6:30 or 7:00 P.M. It is helpful if you establish your baby's bedtime and plan for it by beginning your prebed routine an hour before, if at all possible.

I often hear about how babies and young children have a "meltdown" period at the end of the day, when they get fussy, whiny, and out of sorts. I now suspect that it's simply a sign of overtired children longing for sleep.

Early to Bed, Early to Rise?

For babies, early to bed does *not* mean early to rise! Most babies sleep better and *longer* with an earlier bedtime. Many parents are afraid to put their baby to bed so early, thinking that they will

> **Mother-Speak**
>
> "One evening we were visiting friends and in all of the excitement we missed the 'window of opportunity' for getting Alicia to sleep. She passed into the 'downright weird window.' She was motoring through the house like a race car with no driver. When I finally convinced her to lie on my lap to nurse, it was like nursing a baby monkey! It took forever for her to settle down and fall asleep."
>
> **Robin, mother of thirteen-month-old Alicia**

then face a 5 A.M. wake-up call. Or they may come home from work and *want* to keep baby up late to play. But keeping your little one up too late backfires, and he becomes overtired, distressed, and too wound up to settle down, and more often, a late night is the one followed by that early morning awakening.

My little Coleton used to go to bed at 9 or 9:30, the time when my older children went to bed, because it was convenient for me. At that time in the evening, it would take him a long time to get settled. I never connected his inability to settle with his late bedtime. When I started putting him to bed between 7:00 and 8:00, he fell asleep much more quickly and slept more soundly. And as an added bonus, I recovered some quality "me" time in the evening that I had long forgotten about. This has been a common experience among my test mommies. Many were truly surprised to find that an earlier bedtime really did help their baby fall asleep easier and faster and often encouraged better sleep and a later waking time.

What About Working Parents?

If you are a working parent, and your evening with your little one *begins* at 6:30 or 7:00, you may find yourself torn between keeping your baby up for some playtime and getting him right to bed.

Because you are reading this book, I know that you would like your baby to sleep better. This is a key idea, so it may be worth trying it out to see what the results are for you.

Some working parents find that when their baby goes to sleep earlier, and sleeps better, he awakens in a pleasant mood, eager to play. Because you, the parent, have gotten a good night's sleep, you can consider getting up earlier in the morning and saving some time before work to play with your baby, as an alternative to that late-evening play session. You'll both enjoy that special morning time. Later, when your baby is consistently sleeping all night, every night, you can then move bedtime a little later and judge whether the difference affects your baby's sleep.

Finding Your Baby's Best Bedtime

It can take some experimentation to find your baby's best bedtime. If you have been putting your little one to bed too late in the evening, you can approach this adjustment in one of two different ways:

- Adjust your baby's bedtime to be earlier by fifteen to thirty minutes every two or three nights. Pay attention to how easily your baby falls asleep as well as his awakening time and mood to gauge the effectiveness of the changes until you settle on his best bedtime, or
- Beginning at around 6:30 P.M., watch your baby closely. As soon as he exhibits any signs of tiredness, put him right to bed, even if his previous bedtime has been 11:00 P.M. (For a list of the signs, see page 111.) When you do this, keep your home quiet and the baby's room dark so that it resembles his usual environment in the middle of the night. If this bedtime is substantially earlier than usual, your baby may think he's going down for a nap and awaken after a short snooze. If he does this, respond very quickly so that he doesn't fully awaken. Follow your usual method for helping

him fall right back to sleep, such as rocking or nursing; keep the room dark and quiet as you do during the middle of the night. It may take a week or more of adjustment to settle into a new bedtime.

Follow a Flexible Yet Predictable Daytime Routine

This idea may help everyone.

During the first year of life, a baby's biological clock slowly matures. According to Dr. Dement, "As the weeks go by, the baby starts sleeping longer and being awake longer. This is caused by the consolidation of sleep periods. Then, around the fortieth week, the baby has started waking and going to sleep about the same time each day. His biological clock becomes in tune with the twenty-four-hour day."

Yes, you read that correctly. He wrote *the fortieth week*! That's ten months old! In other words, we cannot force a baby to conform to a parent's desire for a pleasant day, a lengthy nap, and a long, uninterrupted night's sleep. We need to make baby's world conducive to sleep in every way we can. We must remove any obstacles to peaceful nighttime sleep, and wait patiently for nature to do what's best. Yes, some babies do consolidate their sleep earlier than forty weeks (lucky you if you had one of those!) and some require longer. (OK, I'll say it—some, much longer.)

Even given the constraints of your baby's natural sleep consolidation schedule, you can help this process along by making sure that when baby wakes in the morning, he is exposed to bright light (preferably natural daylight) and that the hour before sleep at night is dim and quiet. Waking up at about the same time every morning can help set your baby's biological clock, too. Yes, that means that *you* have to get up at the same time every morning, but this will help set *your* biological clock as well as your baby's.

Routine Days, Routine Nights

Keeping a regular feeding, napping, and activity schedule helps set your baby's internal clock. As an example, while you may enjoy sleeping in on the weekends, this can disrupt your baby's regular schedule; he neither knows nor cares what day it is. Any changes to his normal sleeping pattern prevent his biological clock from working properly. (By the way, this is true for adults, too. One of the best ways to treat adult insomnia is to set a wake-up time and adhere to it seven days a week. You can read more about that in Chapter 11.)

As I have said before, I am not suggesting a clock-watching program. Such regimens only put unnecessary stress on you and your baby. Instead, set up a typical daytime routine and adjust it daily based on your baby's cues, your mood, the weather, and any situations that arise. What you want to avoid is a haphazard week of events—awaking Monday morning at 7, Tuesday morning at 9; lunch on Wednesday at 11, on Thursday not until 1; naptime on Monday at 11, on Tuesday at 1. When your schedule (or shall I say, lack of schedule) looks like this, your baby's biological clock isn't able to work properly. It's much better to have a predictable pattern, allowing for flexibility.

Mother-Speak

"I am not big on 'routines,' but with the twins I have had to discipline myself to have somewhat of a routine. I try not to be an avid clock-watcher; instead, I pay attention to the babies' cues. For example, I try to put the babies down for a nap around 9:30. This morning Rebecca was obviously tired at 9:30. Thomas, on the other hand, was in great form, laughing, playing, and enjoying life—not in the least tired. So I put Rebecca down for a nap and kept Thomas up for another thirty minutes. If I had tried to put him down when he wasn't tired, I would have eventually gotten him to sleep, but it would have been a struggle. By waiting thirty minutes, until he showed signs of tiredness, I got him to sleep easily. In other words, I have a vague structure to my day, with some flexibility depending on my babies."

Alice, mother of six-month-old twins Rebecca and Thomas

A daily routine for a two-year-old might look like this: (This is just a rough sample; yours may be very different.)

7:00—Up for the day
Get dressed
Have breakfast
Playtime
11:30–12:00—Lunch
12:00–12:30—Down for a nap
After nap, midday snack
Playtime
5:00—Dinner
6:30–7:00—Bath and start bedtime routine
8:00—Bedtime

When you have a daily eat, sleep, and play routine, you will find that your baby is more willing to nap, eat, and sleep when the regular time comes, because his internal clock ticks along with your predictable schedule. Of course, if your baby is strictly breast- or formula-fed he should be "demand fed" (or a softer description that I prefer: "cue fed") whenever he is hungry. However, you can build a predictable routine flow around the other parts of your day.

Have Your Baby Take Regular Naps

This idea may help everyone.
According to sleep research, and motherly experience, the length and quality of naps affect nighttime sleep. (And conversely, nighttime sleep affects naps.) A nap less than one hour in length does not really count. These catnaps can take the edge off, but because the sleep cycle is not complete, they may just make your baby fussier in the long run. A few babies seem to rewrite this rule and function beautifully on a forty-five-minute nap, but don't assume this to be the case for your baby unless both his nap and nighttime sleep are consistent and he seems well rested.

Mother-Speak
"Now that I am more aware of the importance of naps I try very hard to make sure she has a good nap every day. She really does then sleep better at night. It's amazing what a difference naps make!"

Tina, mother of twelve-month-old Anjali

Babies differ in their needs for nap length and number of naps—but Table 4.1 is a general guide that applies to most babies.

Table 4.1 Average Number and Length of Naps for Babies

Age	Number of naps	Total length of naptime (hours)
4 months	3	4–6
6 months	2	3–4
9 months	2	2½–4
12 months	1–2	2–3
2 years	1	1–2
3 years	1	1–1½
4 years	0	0
5 years	0	0

When Should Your Baby Nap?

Timing of naps is important, too. A nap too late in the day will negatively affect nighttime sleep. Certain times of the day are better for napping because they suit your baby's developing biological clock; these optimum periods balance sleep and wake time to affect night sleep in the most positive way. Again, all babies are different, but generally, best times for naps are as follows:

- If baby takes three naps: midmorning, early afternoon, and early evening
- If baby takes two naps: midmorning and early afternoon
- If baby takes one nap only: early afternoon

If you want your baby to welcome naptime, use the general guidelines already described and watch her signals. Naps should happen *immediately* when she shows signs of tiredness. If you wait too long, she becomes *overtired*, "wired," and unable to sleep. Once you are familiar with your baby's nap needs, you can plan for your nap routine to start the wind-down process. If consistent naps are new to you, look more for your baby's signs of tiredness and scrimp on the routine until you settle into a predictable pattern. In other words, don't begin a lengthy prenap routine if your baby is clearly ready to sleep.

Watch for these signs of fatigue; your baby may demonstrate one or more of these:

- Decreasing activity
- Quieting down
- Losing interest in people and toys
- Rubbing eyes
- Looking "glazed"
- Fussing
- Yawning
- Lying down on the floor or on a chair
- Caressing a lovey or asking for a pacifier, a bottle, or to nurse

This timing is very, very important! You have probably experienced this scenario: Your baby looks tired and you think, "Time for a nap." So you wash her hands and face, change her diaper, answer a phone call, put out the dog, and head for your baby's crib, only to find that she's suddenly wide awake and eager to play! What happened? She has moved through her window of tiredness and gotten that "second wind" that buys her another hour of two of alert time before she reenters her tired state. This can often happen later in the day. Suddenly your baby is (finally!) ready for a nap at dinnertime, and the plot thickens—do you put her down for a late nap and thus extend bedtime, or keep her awake and deal with a tired, fussy baby? Rather than face this ordeal, respond earlier to her signs of fatigue and get her in for her nap right at that time.

Once you have watched your baby carefully for a week or so, you should be able to create a nap schedule that works with her daily periods of alertness and tiredness, thus making your nap schedule easy to adhere to.

The Nap Routine

Once you've established a nap schedule for your baby, create a simple but specific nap routine that is different from your night-time routine. It can have similarities that signal sleep, for example, the presence of a lovey or special sleep-inducing music. Follow your nap routine the same way every day. (Except, as I mentioned before, if your baby is showing clear signs of being tired and ready to sleep. Then abbreviate or even eliminate your routine for that day.)

For a reluctant napper, your routine may include some relaxing motion (rocking, relaxing in a swing, or walking in a sling or stroller) or gentle lullaby music.

A nap routine doesn't have to be long and involved to be effective. If your baby's nap occurs about the same time every day, many subtle cues—such as the timing of his lunch—will tell your baby that nap time is nearing.

> **Mother-Speak**
> "Our nap routine includes reading two books, then nursing, then rocking with our sleep music playing. It's short, but it works."
>
> **Amber, mother of nine-month-old Nathaniel**

Important: If you are working on solving a frequent night-waking problem, do *anything* and *everything* that works to get your baby to nap during the day; a well-rested baby will respond better to the nighttime sleep ideas.

Getting the Short Napper to Sleep Longer

Some babies will show you their tired signs and go down for a nap rather easily, but then, twenty minutes or so later, they're up again. Most parents resign themselves to this short nap routine.

Nathaniel, nine months old

What appears to be happening is that your baby moves through her sleep cycle and she awakens fully when she hits her first brief awakening. (Remember this from Chapter 2?) The key to getting your short napper to lengthen her naps is to help her go right back to sleep. This is how it works.

Put your baby down for a nap. Set a timer or keep your eye on the time. About five or ten minutes *before* the usual awakening time, sit outside the bedroom door and listen carefully. (Use this time to read a book, knit, or do some other peaceful, pleasant activity. Or be practical and fold laundry or pay your bills.) The minute your baby makes a sound, go in quickly. You'll find him in a sleepy, just-about-to-wake-up state. Use whatever technique helps him fall back to sleep—breastfeeding, rocking, or offering a bottle or pacifier. If you've caught him quickly enough, he will fall back to sleep. After a week or so of this intervention, your short napper should be taking a much longer snooze without any help from you.

Help Your Baby Learn How to Fall Asleep Without Help

🌟 **This idea may help everyone.**

As we discussed in Chapter 2, everyone has night wakings. If your baby is waking *you* up frequently at night, the problem is *not* the awakenings, but that she doesn't know how to go back to sleep on her own. There are ways to help your baby feel comfortable and secure when she wakes up so that she can go back to sleep without your help.

"My Bed Is a Nice Place!"

This first idea helps your baby learn that her bed is a safe, comfortable place.

Spend some quiet, cuddly time during the day in the place you want your baby to sleep at night. Read, talk, sing, and play. Have two or three of these very pleasant interludes during the day with Baby in her sleeping place. If your baby responds positively, try to get her interested in watching a mobile or playing with a toy as you fade back and sit quietly in a chair beside her and watch.

By following these steps your baby will come to know her crib as a welcoming, safe, and comfortable haven. It will become familiar. She will find comfort in waking there during the night

---

Mother-Speak

"As you suggested, we played with Dylan in his crib so he could get used to it. He has this really cool mobile that he loves and we let him 'play' with it two or three times a day. This has really helped him get used to his crib. I think that's one of the reasons he is starting to put himself to sleep when he wakes up during the night."

Alison, mother of five-month-old Dylan

and find it easier to go back to sleep. (This is an especially important idea if you've attempted to let your baby cry it out in the past. It can help banish any negative memories and replace them with a sense of peacefulness about being in the crib.)

Falling Asleep in Different Ways

Right now, your baby may fall asleep in only one way, such as nursing, rocking, or having a bottle. This activity is a very powerful signal that your baby associates with falling asleep. It is so powerful that he may believe that the only way he *can* fall asleep is when this signal is present.

Mother-Speak

"Emma has always fallen asleep breastfeeding. Once in a while my sister baby-sits her while my husband and I go out. It never fails that she'll be wide awake when we get home, no matter how late. My sister says she tries everything, but the little stinker waits until I walk in the door. Two minutes of nursing and she's sound asleep."

Lorelie, mother of six-month-old Emma

If your baby relies on one specific signal to fall asleep, you can help her change this association and learn that she can fall asleep in different ways.

If you choose to follow this suggestion, creating and following nap- and bedtime routines prior to sleep, as discussed earlier in this chapter, will help. But the final step occurs in different places.

Usually, it's easier to begin this plan with naps before tackling nighttime. Does your baby fall asleep in the car or swing? While rocking, using a pacifier, or walking in the stroller? Find and use

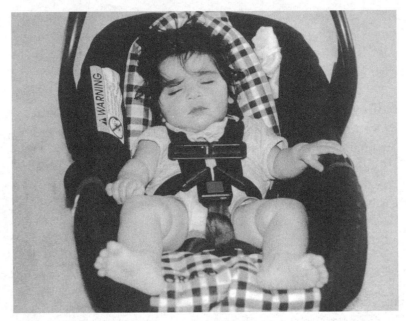

Areesa, eight months old

alternative ways to help your baby to fall asleep for naps. If possible, use two methods. Try to get her comfortable with a variety of ways to fall asleep. One day, go for a ride in the car. The next day, put her in a swing. The third day, rock her. After you have done this for a week or more, you can begin to use your alternate "signals" to bring your baby to a very sleepy state, and then move her quietly to her bed.

At this point, stay with your baby, and pat or touch her in the way that is soothing. If you have been using a nap routine and watching her signals, she should then be able to fall asleep on her own. If she doesn't, go ahead and use the method that works best. Your goal, after all, is for your baby to take a nap.

You may then gradually shorten your routine until it is comfortable for both of you. Once your nap schedule is in place, and your nighttime sleep is settling down, you can eliminate all those alternate methods for falling asleep and use the one that is most convenient for you.

Introduce a Lovey

This idea may help everyone.

Some babies attach themselves to a blanket or toy that becomes a "lovey." This is a transitional object that comforts your baby in your absence. In some cases, you may be able to help your baby become attached to a lovey or comfort object so that he has something to cuddle and help him fall asleep without your help.

A lovey does *not* take your place. Instead, it is something that your baby can use to feel safe when you are not with her. Interestingly, only one of my children discovered her own lovey: my award-winning-sleeper baby, Vanessa. Appropriately enough, her lovey was a red pillowcase named Pilly. Oh, did I say *was*? At twelve years old, Pilly still holds a place of honor in her bedroom, functioning not so much as a lovey, but as a sweet reminder of when she was little. Angela and David had favorite cuddly toys, but none that would qualify as a lovey. With Coleton, I was able to encourage his attachment to a lovey. It wasn't nearly as intense as with Vanessa, but it became a sleep cue and was a helpful piece of the whole sleep plan that I created for him.

Some children adopt a lovey in babyhood and continue to use it all through childhood. Others switch to a new lovey from time to time, other children find solace in any soft, fuzzy toy, and some never do take to the idea of a lovey. You'll be able to tell which category your child fits in by watching his actions.

Choose a Safe Lovey

Choose a soft toy that your baby is already attracted to, or pick a safe stuffed animal that meets these criteria:

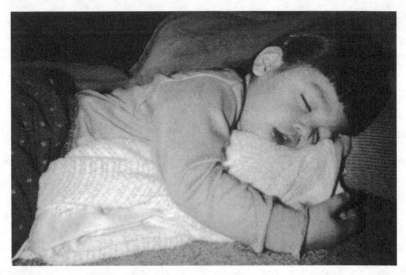

Emily, twenty-four months old

- No button eyes or nose, nor any small, potentially removable pieces
- No clothes, hats, or other removable pieces of fabric
- Firm, not floppy
- Small and easy for baby to hold and manipulate

The ideal lovey is a stuffed animal created especially for babies. For example, I purchased a little flannel doll called a "Snoedel" (snoedel.com) for Coleton. (Please note that I have no affiliation with this business other than as a satisfied customer.) After he became accustomed to having it in bed, he let us know that he was tired by asking for his "noodle." (Or we would encourage him to *get* tired by cuddling him with his "noodle.")

When you have carefully chosen the lovey, place it between the two of you whenever you nurse your baby, give him a bottle, or rock him. At other times of the day, you might even want to "wear" this lovey inside your shirt for a few hours to give it that lovely Mommy (or Daddy) smell, because babies can recognize their parents' scents. At first, it is best to use this lovey only at sleep times so it becomes one of the sleep-time cues.

You can introduce a lovey at any age. If your baby is young, you can choose something yourself, and gauge baby's response to the toy. As your baby gets older, she will have a definite say in determining which toy attracts and soothes her; this is evident anytime you see a child wandering around with a well-worn blanket, a hairless teddy bear, or a scrap of Mommy's old nightie. When your baby becomes a toddler, you may find that he will expand the usefulness of this lovey by holding onto it whenever he needs a little extra security. So if you have any say in the matter, do direct your child toward something that you'll enjoy having in the family for years to come.

If baby does indeed get attached to this lovey, be sure to buy at least two to prevent any lost-lovey disasters—or at least choose one that's easily replaceable or commercially available.

Mother-Speak

"I finally found a lovey that I like for Carrson, and he likes it also. When we hold it between us when we nurse, he plays with it and talks to it. It's becoming a 'friend.'"

Pia, mother of eight-month-old Carrson

Make Night Sleeping Different from Daytime Naps

This idea may help everyone.

When your baby wakes up, he doesn't know if he's waking from a nap or from nighttime sleep, so you need to differentiate the two for him. You can help your baby stay in a sleepy state all night by keeping nighttime quiet and dark. These are some ways to make night sleeping unique:

- When your baby wakes in the night, do not talk. Say "shhhh" or "night night," but refrain from conversation.
- Do not turn on any lights. Even a twenty-five-watt bulb can trigger your baby's biological clock to signal "wake-up time." (Use a low-wattage night-light if you need one.)
- Keep your activity slow and quiet.
- Put your baby in absorbent nighttime diapers with lots of ointment. Change only a soiled or very wet diaper or if baby desires a change. Every diaper change will wake up your baby and reinforce night waking. (Think of it this way: when your baby is sleeping through the night, you won't be getting up to change your sleeping baby's diaper, will you? Also, as your baby is waking up less to nurse or have a bottle, his diaper won't get as wet.) When you do change a diaper, have all your supplies organized and close by so that you can do it quickly. And make certain you use a warm wipe on that sleepy bottom, since a cold, wet washcloth is a sure way to wake your baby up.
- If you have windows that let evening or early morning light in, cover them up with something dark or opaque, like light-blocking blinds, thick curtains, or even a temporary

Mother-Speak

"I have always had this approach, simply because I am way too tired to change diapers, talk to the baby, or play with the baby at night. It works really well. In the last five years with my four children, I have only rarely been awake for long periods deep in the night with a baby. Many of my friends have this problem on a daily basis. But for me, even with night-waking twins, I am far better rested than they because my babies go back to sleep so quickly."

Alice, mother of six-month-old twins Rebecca and Thomas

shield of cardboard. (Leave the covers off during daytime naps.)

- Keep activity toys out of the sleeping area. One stuffed animal or your baby's lovey should be the only toy in his bed. When baby wakes during the night, you don't want the notion of playtime entering his little mind. Like loveys and routines, the presence of toys is a cue—but of the wrong kind for this hour.

Develop Key Words as a Sleep Cue

⭐ **This idea may help everyone.**

You can condition your baby to know it is sleep time when you say certain words in a certain way. Begin now by deciding what your sleep-association words will be. The standard quiet sound of "shhh" is often helpful because it resembles the sound that your baby heard in the womb. Your key words can be something like a whispered "shhh, shhh, it's OK, sleepy time." Or "night night, shhh, shhh, night night." Or, "Enough, already, just go to sleep!" (I'm obviously kidding on that one, although I remember distinctly saying that to Coleton one night.) An alternative to establishing key words is to quietly hum a special relaxing melody.

Once you decide on your key words, get your baby accustomed to them by saying them each time your baby is quiet, peaceful, and falling asleep. Once your baby is familiar with the words, use them to settle him at bedtime or if he wakes during the night.

How to Introduce Your Key Words

For the first few weeks, use your key words only when baby is actually falling asleep. You want your key words to be associated with her sleepy state. *Do not* use the key words when Baby is crying or unhappy, as *that* is what she will associate the words with. Funny enough, I learned this from my dog trainer! Yes, *dog trainer*. She says most people say, "No barking" when their dog

Mother-Speak

"My husband, Royce, is now very familiar with using our key words, 'shhh, shhh, time for night night' when he goes to put Kyra back to sleep. Well, if he hears her cry on the baby monitor during the night, I'll often hear him say, 'shhh, shhh, time for night night.' As if Kyra could hear him through the bedroom wall! Each morning I ask him what he was thinking, and he sincerely does not remember doing it."

Leesa, mother of nine-month-old Kyra

is barking, so the dog thinks that "No barking" is an order to bark! She suggests saying it when the dog is in a quiet state so he associates the command with quiet. I heard something similar from motivational speaker Tony Robbins in a lecture on word association. He suggested repeating words such as "relax" when you are feeling relaxed, so that you can replicate your relaxed stage when you are in stressful situations. So, at first, use your key words when your baby is in a quiet, nearly asleep state. Later, when the association is made, you can use your key words to help him calm down and fall asleep.

Use Music or Sound as Sleep Cues

This idea may help everyone.

As a complement to—or instead of—the key words strategy, a soft lullaby music tape at nap- and bedtime when Baby is falling asleep may do. Indeed, recent research indicates that soft bedtime music causes many babies to relax and fall asleep more easily. Choose the bedtime music carefully, though. Some music (including jazz and some classical music) is too complex and stimulating. Pick simple, repetitive, predictable music, like traditional lullabies. Tapes created especially for putting babies to sleep are great choices. Pick something that *you* will enjoy listening to night after night, too. (Using a tape player with an automatic repeat function is helpful for keeping the music going as long as you need it to play.)

Tapes that play sounds of nature are widely available and very lovely. They may work nicely, as well as small sound-generating or white-noise devices and clocks you may have seen in stores. The nature sounds (raindrops, a babbling brook, or running water) often are similar to your heartbeat and fluids rushing in and out of the placenta, which is what your baby heard in utero. (Remember those sounds from when you listened to your baby's heartbeat with the Doppler stethoscope?) A ticking clock or bubbling fish tank are also wonderful white-noise options.

> **Mother-Speak**
> "I went out today and bought a small aquarium and the humming noise does seem to relax Chloe and help her to sleep. I didn't buy any fish though. Who has time to take care of fish when you're half asleep all day?"
>
> **Tanya, mother of thirteen-month-old Chloe**

You can find some suitable tapes and CDs made especially for babies or others that are made for adults to listen to when they want to relax. Whichever you pick, listen to it first and ask yourself, "Does this relax me? Would it make me feel sleepy if I listened to it in bed?"

If you put your baby to sleep in a noisy, active house full of people, keeping the tape running (auto rewind) will help mask baby-waking noises like dishes clanking, people talking and laughing, TV, or dogs barking. This can also help transition your sleeping baby from a noisy daytime house to which he's become accustomed subconsciously to one of absolute nighttime quiet.

Once your baby is familiar with your key words, calming noise, or music, you can use them to help your baby fall back to sleep when he wakes up in the middle of the night. Simply soothe him by saying your key words or playing the music (very quietly) during the calming and falling asleep time. If he wakes and cries, repeat this process.

If your baby gets used to his sleep-time sounds you can take the tape with you if you will be away from home for nap- or bed-time. The familiarity of these sounds will help your baby sleep in an unfamiliar environment.

Eventually your baby will rely on this technique less and less to fall and stay asleep. You can help this process along by lowering the volume a small amount every night until you finally don't turn the music or sounds on at all.

Change Your Baby's Sleep Association

This idea may help frequent breastfeeders, frequent night-time bottle-feeders, and pacifier users.

Your baby has learned to associate sucking (having your nipple or his bottle or pacifier in his mouth) with sleeping. I have heard a number of sleep experts refer to this as a "negative sleep association." I certainly disagree, and so would my baby. It is probably the most positive, natural, pleasant sleep association a baby can have.

Frequent Breastfeeders

The problem with the association of breastfeeding to sleep is not the association but our busy lives. If you had nothing whatsoever to do besides take care of your baby, this would be a very pleasant way to pass your days until she naturally outgrew the need. However, in our world, few parents have the luxury of putting everything else in their lives on hold until their baby gets older. With this in mind, I will give you a number of ideas so that you can gradually, and *lovingly*, help your baby learn to fall asleep without this very wonderful and powerful sleep aid.

Frequent Bottle-Feeding Babies

Your baby should be weaned from the need to have a bottle for sleep for a number of reasons. First, when your baby falls asleep with a bottle, the formula or juice might puddle in her mouth as she falls asleep and cause nursing bottle caries (cavities) syndrome. (Although less of a risk, this can also happen with a breastfed baby who always sleeps while nursing.)

The second concern with using a bottle as a sleep aid is that your baby may not be hungry, but craves the sucking sensation to fall asleep. Therefore, she will be drinking more than she really needs.

The third issue is that it's simply no fun to be preparing and serving bottles all night when you'd much rather be sleeping!

Should You Use a Pacifier?

The jury continues to be out on whether pacifier use is a good or a bad thing, but around 50 percent of parents do give their babies pacifiers, because they work so well to help a baby stay calm and relaxed. Generally, pacifier use from about three months of age to about age two is considered an acceptable practice. Prior to three months, pacifier use may interfere with the establishment of breastfeeding, and after age two, it may be associated with dental problems or speech delays. Within that middle age range,

Mother-Speak

"He does sleep with six binkies, but that doesn't bother me because he sleeps all night long. We'll wean him eventually, but for now I enjoy getting a full night's sleep."

Jennifer, mother of six-month-old Coby

many parents are comfortable letting their baby sleep with a pacifier. If this is true in your family, and if your baby is easily comforted back to sleep by his pacifier, you may decide to use this as
a self-soothing method.

Parents in this situation have reported to me that placing several pacifiers around the crib, and helping baby to find them in
the middle of the night, effectively helps baby to go back to sleep
without a parent's intervention. (Always purchase safe, sturdy
one-piece pacifiers, and never attach one to your baby or the crib
in any way.) If you do choose this option, just keep in mind that,
while some babies give up the pacifier on their own, sometime
down the road you probably will be working to wean your baby
from it.

If you decide that you'd rather eliminate your baby's reliance
on a pacifier (or if you'd like to give it a try) read on.

How to Diminish the Sucking-to-Sleep Association

When your baby wakes looking for his bottle, his pacifier, or to
nurse, you most likely replace the pacifier or nurse him back
to sleep. The problem here is that your baby's strong sleep
association most likely will not change without your help. (See
Chapter 2.)

To take the steps to change your baby's sleep association, you
must complicate night wakings for a week or even a month, but
in the long run you can wean your baby from using her pacifier,
her bottle, or your breast as her only nighttime association. In
other words, be prepared to disrupt your own nights for a while
to make some important, worthwhile long-term changes.

Pantley's Gentle Removal Plan

When your baby wakes, go ahead and pop his pacifier or his bottle in his mouth, or nurse him. But, instead of leaving him there
and going back to bed, or letting him fall asleep at the breast, let
him suck for a few minutes until his sucking slows and he is

relaxed and sleepy. Then break the seal with your finger and gently remove the pacifier or nipple.

Often, especially at first, your baby then will startle and root for the nipple. Try to very gently hold his mouth closed with your finger under his chin, or apply pressure to his chin, just under his lip, at the same time rocking or swaying with him. (Use your key words if you have developed them.) If he struggles against this and roots for you or his pacifier or bottle, or fusses, go ahead and replace the nipple or pacifier, but repeat the removal process as often as necessary until he falls asleep.

How long between removals? Every baby is different, but about ten to sixty seconds between removals usually works. You also should watch your baby's sucking action. If a baby is sucking strongly or swallowing regularly when feeding, wait a few minutes until he slows his pace. By paying attention to your baby's swallowing you can also tell when you have had a letdown reflex. You can try to get your baby to release at that time, but you'll need to stop the flow of milk with your hand, or wait a minute for the flow to subside. Usually, after the initial burst of activity, your baby will slow to a more relaxed "fluttery" pace; this is a good time to begin your removal attempts.

It may take two to five (or even more) attempts, but eventually your baby will fall asleep without the pacifier or nipple in her

Mother-Speak

"We got to calling this the Big PPO (Pantley Pull-Off). At first Joshua would see it coming and grab my nipple tighter in anticipation—ouch! But you said to stick with it, and I did. Now he anticipates the PPO and actually lets go and turns and rolls over on his side to go to sleep! I am truly amazed."

Shannon, mother of nineteen-month-old Joshua

mouth. When she has done this a number of times over a period of days, you will notice the removals are much easier, and her awakenings are less frequent.

Pantley's Gentle Removal Plan looks something like this. (This example shows a breastfeeding baby, but the plan is the same whether Baby is breastfeeding, using a bottle, or using a pacifier.)

Baby is awake and nursing vigorously.
Baby's eyes close, and his sucking rate slows.
You gently remove your nipple.
Baby roots (moving his open mouth toward you).
You try holding his chin, but he'll have none of that!
You put him back to the breast.
Count: one thousand, two thousand, . . . ten thousand.*
You gently remove your nipple.
Baby roots.
You try stalling, but no dice.
You put him back to the breast.
Count: one thousand, two thousand, . . . ten thousand.
You gently remove your nipple.
Baby roots.
You put him back to the breast.
Count: one thousand, two thousand, . . . ten thousand.
You gently remove your nipple.
Baby moves a little, and you gently hold his mouth closed.
Baby doesn't resist; he is nearly out.
You place Baby in bed.
He goes to sleep.

---

*The counting is really more for you, to give you a gauge to measure your time and a way to keep yourself calm during your repeated attempts. You can be flexible as you figure out what time spacing works best for you and your baby.

Repeat this process every night until Baby learns she can fall asleep without nursing, sucking a bottle, or using her pacifier. If your baby is a "good napper," you can use the technique for putting her to sleep at naptime, too.

If your baby doesn't nap well, don't trouble yourself with trying too hard to use the removal technique during the day for naps. Remember that good naps mean better nighttime sleep—and better nighttime sleep means better naps. It's a circle. Once you get your baby sleeping better at night, you can then work on the naptime sleep—although once you solve the nighttime association, the naptime sleep may solve itself.

The most important time to use the Pantley's Gentle Removal Plan is the first falling asleep of the night. Often the way your baby falls asleep will affect the rest of his awakenings for the night. I suspect that this is because of the sleep-association affect that I explained earlier when we discussed basic sleep facts. It seems that the way in which your baby falls asleep for the night is how he expects to remain all night long.

Because we want no crying, this is not a one-day solution. But within ten days, as you gently break this strong sleep association, you should see a major reduction in the number of your baby's night wakings.

Changing Your Routine

Very often we parents have a routine we have followed with our babies since birth. The final step before sleep is often nursing or having a bottle. Some babies, like my Coleton, can continue this pattern and still sleep through the night. Others, though, need to have the final step in their routine changed before they begin to sleep all night without needing your help to fall back to sleep. What you'll want to do is take an objective look at your final steps in putting your baby to sleep and make some changes if necessary.

You may want to use massaging, cuddling, or the key words idea (pages 121–122) to help get your baby back to sleep. Eventually the key words and a loving pat will take over for nursing or bottle-feeding, and then that too will fade away, and your baby will be sleeping longer. Here's what one test mommy reported:

Mother-Speak

"I have changed the way I'm putting Carlene to sleep and it's working! Instead of nursing her down, I just feed her until she is relaxed and then I just let her do whatever she wants in the very dim room with me. When she rubs her eyes and looks sleepy I put her in her crib. I used to go out of the room, hoping she would drift off herself, but she would just get agitated and work herself up until I came back. But now, I just stay there. I stand next to the crib, and encourage her to sleep. I say my key words, 'Shhh, it's night-night time, close your eyes sleepy girl,' and I tell her that it's OK to go to sleep. I rub her head or her tummy. She shuts her eyes right when I do this. She'll open them back up a few times, but eventually she settles. Since I'm not nursing or rocking, she is falling asleep without these, so when she lightly wakes during sleep cycle transition, she is finally able to go back to sleep without me. It's been a major breakthrough."

Rene, mother of seven-month-old Carlene

Help Your Baby to Fall Back to Sleep on His Own While You Continue to Breastfeed and Co-Sleep

⭐ **This idea may help breastfeeding and co-sleeping babies.** Let me start by saying that, when you breastfeed and co-sleep, you may find that your baby will wake more often than if she were in a crib down the hall. But you may feel that the reasons that you keep your baby in your bed outweigh the inconvenience of a few night wakings. Like you, I have chosen to breastfeed and co-sleep for many reasons that are important to me—and I've done it with all four of my babies. (If you haven't already, I suggest you read *Attachment Parenting* by Katie Granju and Betsy Kennedy, Pocket Books, 1999. This is a lovely book that will help you understand and enjoy the choices you make in regard to where and how your baby sleeps.)

One important thing to remember is that "this too shall pass." All of my children eventually slept through the night, and your baby will too. However, there are ways that you can speed up the process of your baby sleeping all night—even while keeping your little one in bed with you.

Make sure that you've read the safety list in Chapter 1. Much of what I have read about the dangers associated with co-sleeping point to unsafe sleeping environments as the real issue. Read up on the topic and make a wise and informed decision, and religiously follow all safety measures.

Mother-Speak

"I am not ready to move Atticus out of my bed. I enjoy having him near me at night and snuggling with him. I slept with my daughter Gracie when she was a baby and she transitioned quite easily when we were both ready. Bedtime has always been a time of comfort for her and I feel that when the time is right for Atticus he will be much the same. Even so, it would be nice to have him waking up less often to nurse."

**Pam, mother of eleven-month-old Atticus and
five-year-old Gracie**

The challenge with breastfeeding and co-sleeping mother-baby pairs is that each partner is so in tune with the other that the slightest movement or noise will have both awake. Mommy and Daddy end up creating additional wakings in between the baby's natural ones, thus creating an all night wake-sleep pattern.

The trick is to get Baby accustomed to sleeping beside you but able to go back to sleep without your help (typically in the form of nursing). You can do this by shortening your nighttime help routines. I know that this is possible because today my son Coleton is eighteen months old—still breastfeeding and co-sleeping—and sleeping ten hours at night without a peep. This is the same baby that a few months ago woke up every hour or so to breastfeed. So I am living proof that you don't have to give up a sleeping ritual that you love just to get some sleep. Not all babies will respond as Coleton did, of course. But many of my test mommies practice breastfeeding and co-sleeping, and many found their own sleep success without having to move their babies out of their beds. Some stubborn little ones do require a move to another room before they will give up the luxury of nighttime nursing, but do try all of my ideas for a few weeks before you assume this to be correct for your baby. (If you decide it's time to move Baby out of your bed, you'll find ideas for a gentle, peaceful transition in the section beginning on page 137.)

When Baby wakes, you probably have a routine to get her back to sleep. For Coleton and me, it was breastfeeding. I used to nurse him until he was totally asleep; the nipple literally would fall out of his mouth. Every hour, we had a very exact pattern. Coleton woke, I shifted him to the other side, I kissed his head, he nursed—a beautiful, soothing ritual. Sometimes he would wake up and pucker up, looking for the kiss and the shift. As sweet as this ritual was, after twelve months of this hourly ceremony, I desperately needed a change.

Stop Feeding a Sleeping Baby

As with the writing of this book, learning how to break the association was a gradual, thoughtful process that required much self-
examination. I found I was responding to Coleton so quickly and
intuitively that I'd put him to the breast before he even made a
real noise—he would just fidget, gurgle, or sniff and I would put
him to the breast. I began to realize that, on so many of these
occasions, he would have gone back to sleep without me.

As you know, I am a follower of the "never let your baby cry"
rule, and I took it very seriously. What I didn't understand,
though, is that babies make sounds *in their sleep*. And these
sounds do *not* mean that Baby needs to nurse. Babies moan,
grunt, snuffle, whimper, and even cry *in their sleep*. Babies can
even nurse *in their sleep*.

The first step to helping your baby sleep longer is to determine
the difference between sleeping noises and awake noises. When
Baby makes a noise, stop. Listen. Wait. Peek. As you listen attentively to her noises and watch her, you will learn the difference
between sleeping snorts and "I'm waking up and I need you now"
noises.

When I learned this eye-opening piece of information, I
started "playing asleep" when Coleton made a nighttime noise. I

Mother-Speak

"Last night he was nursing and I pulled him off and put my finger under his chin like you suggested. I was thinking 'this will
never work, he'll be mad!'—but it worked, he went to sleep!
The other trick is helpful too. When I take him off and then roll
over, he thinks I'm asleep then he goes to sleep, too!"

Carol, mother of nine-month-old Ben

would just listen and watch—not moving a single muscle—until he began to make actual wakeful noises. Some of the time, he never did; he just went back to sleep!

Shorten Your Nighttime Nursing Times

You may be following the pattern that we were—putting your baby to the breast and then both of you falling back to sleep. It's very easy to do, because the act of breastfeeding releases hormones that make Mommy sleepy, just as much as the milk makes Baby sleepy. The problem is that your baby falls soundly asleep at the breast, and begins to believe that having the nipple in her mouth is the only way she *can* sleep. Therefore, every time she reaches a brief awakening, she looks to re-create her sleep-inducing condition. You can help your baby learn to fall asleep without this aid by shortening your nighttime nursing intervals.

When you are sure your baby is awake and looking to nurse, go ahead and nurse him for a short time. Stay awake! And as soon as he slows his pace from the gulping, drinking mode to the slow fluttery comfort nursing, you can gently disengage him while patting him or rubbing him. (See Pantley's Gentle Removal Plan described on pages 126–129.)

Sometimes you can put your baby's hand on your breast during the removal, since many babies will accept this touch as a substitute for nursing; it seems to keep you "connected," and he knows that the milk is nearby if he needs it.

Another option is to make the latch-on a little less comfortable and convenient for your baby. So, instead of laying tummy to tummy with your baby cradled in your arm, shift yourself slightly onto your back so that he has to work a bit to keep the nipple in his mouth. Often he'll decide it's too much effort and he'll let go and go back to sleep.

If your baby whimpers at any point during this removal process, or somehow lets you know he is up for real (by crawling onto your chest, for example!), go ahead and breastfeed him. Then repeat the process to keep the nursing session short, and disconnect him before he is deeply asleep.

Sometimes, it may take three to five times before your baby will settle into sleep. After a week of using this technique with Coleton, he began to disengage *himself*, turn over with his back to me, and fall asleep! It was wonderful; perhaps only a co-sleeping and breastfeeding mommy can understand just how sweet her baby's backside can be at this time. In fact, Coleton (at this writing, eighteen months old) *still* does this; he nurses until he's very comfortable, then rolls away from me and goes to sleep. Now that he's sleeping ten or so hours, I leave him in bed with his brother David in our sleeping room (see photo on page 3), and I am free to join my husband in our own bed for baby-free sleep and couple time.

Move the Milk

Here is another idea especially for co-sleepers. After you nurse your baby, scoot yourself away from her. If she is snuggled right up against you, she will awaken and want to nurse more often—sometimes, as I mentioned earlier, even in her sleep. If your baby is used to feeling you against her, then you may want to try a tactile replacement. A small stuffed animal is perfect for the job. (See pages 117–119.) Simply place the toy next to your baby's body or legs (away from her face) when you move away, so that she feels something against her.

For those persistent night nursers, you may even want to change your sleeping arrangement for a few weeks until you get the frequent night waking under control. I put two mattresses on the floor next to each other in our sleeping room. During the period of change, I began to nurse Coleton on one bed; once he was asleep, I'd move over to the other. Granted, it was only five feet away, but it was far enough away that I did not cause any

Mother-Speak

"I finally realized that I had a hidden fear that if I night weaned her she would day wean too. I didn't want that to happen so I was nursing her no matter the time of day or night. I've modified my thinking and now I nurse her for a long prebed session and a leisurely morning session instead of thinking we need to nurse all night long."

Becky, mother of thirteen-month-old Melissa

additional awakenings. If you have a crib, you can try the side-car arrangement—pushing the crib up next to your bed and letting baby have his own sleeping cubby. (At the risk of sounding like a nag, follow good safety measures if you do this.)

I must tell you though, that some very persistent co-sleeping night wakers have "Mommy radar" and may continue their numerous wakings until Mommy and Baby sleep in different rooms. If you try all of my other ideas, and find that your baby is still waking frequently, you'll need to make that ultimate decision—what's more important right now, co-sleeping or just plain sleeping? I cannot answer that question for you, and there is no right answer. You'll need to examine the needs of every member of your family to determine just what path you should take. Even if you decide to move your baby to a different sleeping spot, remember that, when he is sleeping solidly through the night, you can welcome him back into your bed anytime.

You may also want to use your key words to help get your baby back to sleep. (See pages 121–122.) Eventually, the key words and loving touch will take over for nursing, and then that too will fade away, and your baby will sleep longer without waking you.

Just like most of the ideas in this book, the one here is based on gradual change over time—no quick fixes or tearful transitions.

Help Your Baby Fall Back to Sleep on His Own and Move Him out of Your Bed and into His Own

This idea may help co-sleeping babies move to a crib.
Whether you've had your baby in bed with you full-time or part-time, one month or two years, a time may come when you're ready to move Baby out of your bed and into her own. The following is a list of ideas for making this transition. After reviewing them, formulate your strategy by choosing those that best fit your family's unique situation.

Some parents decide to wait until their child is ready to make the move on his own. This is perfectly fine; if you are in no hurry to make a change, then, by all means, enjoy this time! Let the process happen naturally. These ideas are not meant to imply that Baby *should* be in his own bed if this is not what you want; rather, they are here for those parents who have decided that they would like to move Baby to his own bed.

Keep in mind that, in most cases, you don't have to make the change overnight. Often, taking a few weeks, or even a few months, is the most peaceful route. On the other hand, if one or both parents don't have the desire or patience to wait, you *can* make the move quickly, and still be sensitive to your baby's needs.

No matter what you decide, remember that your baby has truly enjoyed nights in your bed, and she won't like sleeping alone at first. Try to make the transition as easy for her as you can.

Make a check by those ideas that appeal to you. Review them and think about them, and then create your own plan to move Baby out of your family bed.

Staying Close but Not Too Close

Place a mattress or pad on the floor near your bed. Put your baby to sleep on the pad, and then climb back up into your bed. If baby wakes to breastfeed or needs a cuddle, bottle, or reassurance, Mommy or Daddy can move down to baby, parent him back to sleep, and get back up in the big bed so the child gets used to sleeping alone. After a week or so of this arrangement, move this same pad or mattress to your baby's room. (You can also do this in reverse, leaving baby in the big bed while you sleep on the pad or mattress.) Again—follow all safety precautions.

Create a Miniature Family Bed

Most co-sleeping babies will sleep fine *anywhere* with Mommy or Daddy sleeping alongside. You can use this to your advantage when moving your baby toward independent sleeping.

If your baby is old enough—more than ten months old or so—place a mattress on the floor in Baby's bedroom. Make sure the room is perfectly childproof and follow all the precautions in Chapter 1.

Use your usual going-to-sleep routine, but instead of sleeping in the big bed, go to sleep with your baby in his own room. For the first few nights, you might want to stay there all night long so your baby gets comfortable with the change.

After a few nights, you can get up and go to your own room after your baby is asleep. If your baby has a lovey or small stuffed animal, place it in your spot when you leave. Keep a baby monitor turned on, and when your baby wakes during the night, quickly go to him. He will discover that you're never very far away and will begin to wake less at night.

The Traveling Crib

If you have a crib for your baby and would like him to sleep in his room, in his crib, try this step-by-step approach. Follow each step from two nights to a week or more, depending on how comfortable you and your baby are at each step.

1. Place the crib right next to your bed in a sidecar arrangement. You can keep the rail that faces your bed down to its lowest setting, or remove it all together. (Important: keep the crib tightly secured to your bed so that it doesn't move and create a gap that could trap your baby.) Special cribs are available for this purpose—for example, the Arm's Reach co-sleeper, available through many baby furniture sources.

   If your baby has always slept nestled against you, you can make this transition a bit easier if you put your scent on the baby's crib sheet. You can sleep on the crib sheet for a few nights, perhaps using it as a pillowcase, or tuck it inside your nightgown for a few hours before bedtime.

2. Once Baby is comfortable with this new arrangement, you can put the fourth side up on the crib and move it just a foot or two away from your bed. Your baby will hear, smell, and see you, but you won't be waking each other with your nocturnal movements, and he will begin to get comfortable sleeping alone.

3. Move the crib to the other side of your bedroom, as far away from your bed as your room allows.

4. Move the crib to baby's bedroom, keeping a monitor turned on so that you can go to your baby quickly if she awakens. After you do this the first few nights, she will be confident that you will be there if she needs you, and she will begin to sleep longer stretches.

The Sneaky Way

Let your baby fall asleep in your bed as always. As soon as she is completely asleep, carry her into her room and put her into her crib. Have a baby monitor turned on so that you can go to her quickly if she wakes up. When she wakes, nurse her in a chair, or bring her to bed to nurse, but then take her back to her crib when she is again asleep.

If you use this technique, you can expect to be traveling the hallway between rooms for a while until the transition is complete. Many babies will adjust rather quickly and will sleep much longer stretches than when they were in bed with another person whose night movements caused extra awakenings. You might even set a time that you'll stop the transfer. For example, move baby to her crib for every awakening until 3:00 A.M., and then just keep her in bed with you after that time so you can get some sleep.

Like all of my ideas, this is not meant to be a rigid, do-it-or-else proposition. You can work with this idea for a few weeks, making the change more peaceful for both you and your baby. (Of course, if you want baby moved pronto, you *could* be very persistent and move through the transition more quickly; that's entirely up to you.)

This idea will work better if you can spend a few pleasant playtimes entertaining Baby while she lies in her crib during the day. This will help her to be comfortable in her crib setting so that, when she wakes there during the night, it will be familiar to her.

For Your Walking, Talking Toddler

If your little one is old enough to understand, and sleeps in a bed (rather than a crib), you can begin the night by putting your child to bed in her own room and explaining what will happen if she wakes up. Set up a "sleeping spot" in your room: a mattress or pad near your bed. Explain to your child that if she wakes up during the night, she can come to her special little bed and go right back to sleep. Explain that Mommy and Daddy need to sleep, so she should tiptoe in as quiet as a mouse and get herself settled without waking you. If she does succeed with this plan, make sure that you praise her a great deal the next morning.

When you use this idea, making a big production about setting up her "big girl" bedroom can be helpful. You may want to rearrange the room, buy new sheets or pillows, and line up lots of friendly stuffed animals. You can leave a sippy cup of water on her nightstand and a flashlight or anything else that might help or comfort her in the middle of the night.

As part of this process, make sure that your bedtime routine is long enough to be relaxing, and that it includes pleasant activities like book reading and a back rub. Your child should land in her bed feeling peaceful and ready to sleep, with the knowledge that she can come into your room if she needs to.

Some children can be convinced to stay in their own beds if promised a reward at the end of the week. For example, "If you stay in your bed all week, you can sleep with Mommy and Daddy on Saturday night." Granted, like many parenting ideas, you need to think about this before you try it. This one may not work for you in particular, and may even backfire, causing your little one to crave the family bed every night. This is a good time for me to remind you that you should not only take into account your particular child's disposition and family situation, but that you should feel free to take bits of my ideas here and formulate your

reativity. You know your own family best, and I
)gether, we can help your baby to sleep all night!

Create a ┘ling Bed

If your baby is more than eighteen months old, and if you have an older child who would welcome the idea, move your baby from your bed to the sibling's bed (being sure, of course, to take all safety precautions outlined in Chapter 1).

We've used the sibling bed idea in our family and find that our children truly enjoy sleeping together. Other parents who use this arrangement agree that it helps decrease sibling rivalry and fighting. I suspect that those late-night and early-morning cuddles and chats keep siblings close.

A sibling bed arrangement can also include some "bed hopping." The kids can decide each night where they would like to sleep, taking turns being the host for the evening. If you do use the sibling bed idea, you'll find that over time your children will begin to sleep separately—first one night, then two, and soon they'll settle into their own beds, on their own. (Many will continue to have "sleepovers" in each other's rooms for years after that, maintaining the special connection that a sibling bed creates.)

Help Your Baby Fall Back to Sleep with Another Person's Assistance

This idea may help breastfeeding and co-sleeping babies.
In most cases, breastfeeding and co-sleeping babies wake up because they love having access to Mommy all night long. Anytime they wake up, they see, hear, smell, and feel you and think, "Aha! Lovely warm milk and a cozy mommy. Gotta have it!" So, if you have a husband, partner, mother, or someone else who is

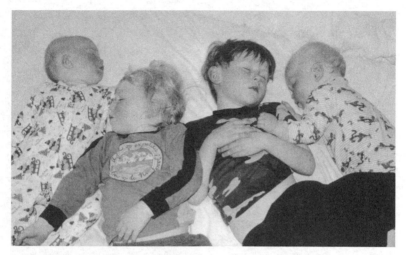

Rebecca, ten months old; Carolyn, three years old;
Patrick, five years old; Thomas, ten months old

willing and able to help for a week or so, you might want to ask
that person to sleep near your baby in your stead.

If your baby is younger than about eighteen months, set up a
crib, cradle, or mattress right next to the helper's bed, as it's *never*
a good idea for someone other than Mom to sleep right next to
a tiny baby; only Mom has that "mother's instinct" that prevents
rolling over on the baby. This should be a person your baby is
very close to and comfortable with. If possible, have him or her
start this process with naps for a few days first. (If not, that's
OK—start right in with bedtime.)

When Baby awakens, have your helper rock, walk with, hum
to the baby—anything that helps her go back to sleep. Try to
avoid using a bottle, as you'll just substitute one "sleeping crutch"
for another. If your helper uses a pacifier to calm baby, keep in
mind that at some point down the road you'll probably have to

Mother-Speak

"I found it virtually impossible to soothe my daughter back to sleep without the breast. She would just get agitated and angry. Our answer was to have Daddy go to her when she woke up to resettle her. The first few nights she was quite irritated that it was Daddy and not Mommy coming to her beck and call. But, by the end of the week, she was totally in love with her Daddy. My husband still says that helping to night wean her (though he was sleep deprived at the time) was one of the most important ways he has ever bonded with his little girl. I noticed that closeness in their relationship immediately, and it still hasn't gone away, even though we're long past that time."

Deirdre, mother of nineteen-month-old Violet

deal with weaning from the pacifier. Many parents find that they are comfortable with that scenario.

Tell your helper that it isn't "do or die." In other words, if baby starts to cry and gets upset, or if your helper is losing patience, tell him or her that it's OK to bring the baby to you. And try again with the next waking. When Baby comes to you (notice I said "when," not "if"), follow the ideas in the section called Help Your Baby to Fall Back to Sleep on His Own While You Continue to Breastfeed and Co-Sleep starting on page 130.

Help Baby to Fall Back to Sleep in Her Crib

⭐ *This idea may help crib sleepers.*

It's likely that every time your baby is crying or calling out to you during the night you are doing something to help him to fall back to sleep. To gradually get Baby to go back to sleep without your

Jared and Jarell, seven months old

assistance, you need to shorten these helping routines during the night.

When Baby wakes, you probably have a specific routine to get her back to sleep, such as picking her up, rocking her, nursing her, and giving her a bottle or pacifier. As you read in Chapter 2, your baby thinks she *needs* this routine to go back to sleep. We don't want to go cold turkey and cut out the familiar, nurturing pattern that you have established; that's a sure way to cause stress and tears. Instead, very gradually modify the *length* of your help routine so that you are doing less each night. Eventually, your baby will develop a new routine that doesn't require your presence.

When your baby wakes up, go ahead and use your regular means of getting him back to sleep, but gradually *shorten the duration* and *vary the technique*. So, instead of letting him fall asleep totally, encourage drowsiness and then see if he'll finish falling asleep on his own. If he fusses, repeat the process. This may take three, four, or more attempts the first few nights; and you may even have to abort your mission on some nights. Over a period of a week or two you will see definite progress, which you will evaluate when you do your ten-day logs.

Your nights might now look something like this:

- Baby wakes.
- You pick her up; sit in a chair; and rock, nurse, bottle-feed, or take her to bed with you until she's soundly asleep.
- Then you probably ease her gently into the crib without waking her. When you move baby from your arms to the crib, you do it very slowly and carefully, so as to not wake her.
- Then you creep out of the room and await your next call.

If you are going to use this suggestion, and if your baby uses a pacifier, bottle, or the breast at every night waking, then you will want to incorporate Pantley's Gentle Removal Plan (pages 126– 129) along with the ideas that follow.

I have found that many mothers have been told to respond to their babies immediately and never let them cry. One problem here. "Experts" forget to tell you that babies make sounds *in their sleep*. Babies moan, grunt, snuffle, whimper, and even cry *in their sleep*. Mothers often run to their little ones at the first noise and scoop their babies out of their cribs. I did this with my first baby, fourteen years ago, and I can still remember that sometimes she was asleep in my arms before I even got to the rocking chair to sit down. What I didn't know was that she had never really been awake.

The first step to helping your baby sleep longer is to determine the difference between sleeping noises and awake noises. I'm not suggesting that you ignore a baby's true cries by any means; she may need you, and this is the only way she can communicate this. In fact, when you wait too long and she wakes up fully—crying and yelling—she will find it much harder to fall back to sleep. Rather, keep her door and yours open, or use a baby monitor. When she makes a noise, stop. Listen. Wait. As you listen attentively to her noises, you will learn the difference between sleeping snorts and "I'm waking up and I need you now" noises.

The following sample pattern shows the duration and type of nighttime help being shortened. This is by no means an exact plan, your own method may be quite different, but this will give you an understanding of the concept:

Phase One: Comfort Until Baby's Almost Asleep

Once you determine your baby is really awake, go and get her. Sit in the rocking chair and rock, nurse, or bottle-feed Baby but only until her eyes close, her sucking rate slows, and she's falling asleep. Try not to wait until she is totally asleep. Stand up with her in your arms and rock or sway gently. When you lay her down, keep your arms around her for a few minutes, making gentle rocking motions. (Yes, this can be tough on your back, but it's only temporary.) She will accept the change from your lap to her bed if you don't abruptly "dump" her there. Keep in mind that, when she sleeps on you, you are moving and breathing, while the bed is still and silent. So gentle movement in the transition helps. Once she seems settled, gently slip your arms out from under her. If she stirs, put your hand on her; whisper your key words or turn on the soothing music; and rock, pat, or touch her gently until she's asleep. If she wakes and cries, pick her up, and repeat this process. You may have to do this two, three, four, maybe five times, but that's OK—*really*. If you or your baby get upset at any point, just go ahead and put her to sleep in your usual way and ditch the plan for the moment. Eventually she will get more comfortable with your new routine and she will go to sleep. She will still be depending on you to help her go back to sleep, but because she is finishing the falling-asleep process in her crib, she will be one step closer to being able to put herself to sleep when she wakes in the night.

Remember, you are making a change. It may take a while for this to work, but this beats spending another year or more in a sleep-deprived stupor!

When you feel that your new routine is working, go on to Phase Two.

Mother-Speak

"The first night I tried the 'Pantley Way,' it worked like a charm. I had to take him out of the crib four times and hold him, but after the fourth time he fussed a bit, I rubbed his back and used my key words—he never cried—and he went to sleep until almost 5:00 A.M. That's another success, because it is usually 3:00 or 3:30. Getting him back to sleep after that early waking is another battle we are working on. I know—patience and baby steps!"

Kim, mother of thirteen-month-old Mathieau

Phase Two: Baby's Settled and Sleepy

Sit in your chair and rock, nurse, or bottle-feed Baby until she's *settled* and *sleepy*, but not yet falling *asleep*. Play your sleep-cue music or sounds. Put her in her crib, pat or touch her, and say your key words until she's asleep. If she wakes and cries, pick her up and repeat this process. You may have to do this two, three, four, maybe five times, but that's OK. If you or your baby get upset at any point, just go ahead and put her to sleep in your usual way. As in Phase One, she will become more comfortable with your new routine and will go to sleep. (Yes, I repeated that idea; it's important to give yourself permission to stop the process for the night any time it's not working. You will still see improvement over time.)

When you feel that your new routine is working, go on to Phase Three.

Phase Three: Comfort Without Pickups

When your baby makes waking sounds, go immediately to her, but try not to pick her up; instead, play your music or sounds, pat her, touch her, or put your arms around her in the same ways you have been, until she's asleep. While she's falling asleep, say your key words. If she wakes and cries, go ahead and revert back to

---

Mother-Speak

"We had good success at Phase One and Phase Two, but there's no way she'd have Phase Three. We kept trying though, and just when I was about to give up, lo and behold! One fine night she actually went back to sleep without my taking her out of the crib! That was the turning point. We never made it to Phase Four, because a week later she stopped waking up at all."

Heidi, mother of ten-month-old Elise

Phase Two or even Phase One, but try to make it brief. And repeat this process.

When you feel that your new routine is working, go on to Phase Four.

Phase Four: Soothing Pats

Go immediately to Baby, but try not to pick her up. Play your music or white noise sounds very quietly, pat her, or touch her. Just stand by her crib and say your key words. If she wakes and cries, revert to Phase Three or even Two, but try to make it very brief. Repeat this process.

When you feel that your new routine is working, go on to Phase Five.

Phase Five: Verbally Soothing Baby

Go immediately to Baby's room, and stand in the doorway. Experiment to determine if you need to turn on your music or sounds. Say your key words. If she wakes and cries, revert back to previous phases, but try to make it very brief. And repeat this process.

When you feel that your new routine is working, go on to Phase Six.

Phase Six: Comfort from Outside the Doorway

Go immediately to baby's room, stand *outside* the doorway where she can't see you, and say your key words. If she wakes and cries, revert back to previous phases, but try to make it very brief. Repeat this process.

The idea is to take small, gradual steps toward your goal. This example is not meant as a blueprint for every baby; rather, it's one demonstration of the idea. You'll need to examine your own bedtime rituals and modify them slightly every few nights until you reach your sleeping goal.

Keep in mind that the phases are not meant to be rigid, inflexible steps. Watch your baby. Stay in tune with your own feelings. Follow your heart. Modify your plan and be flexible as you move through the steps. As long as you are gradually moving toward your goal of having your baby sleep all night without your company, you will eventually get there.

Write a Family Bestseller

This idea may help parents of babies who are more than eighteen months old.

Your baby is older now and can understand more things about life. You have most likely begun to teach the words *please* and *thank you*. She probably is able to follow simple instructions, such as, "Please put this on the shelf." Most babies at this age enjoy reading books, especially books with pictures of real babies. Reading books about sleep to your child at bedtime can help. I've found that most of these depict a predictable, typical bedtime routine: play, bath, pajamas, story, bottle or breast, bed. Seeing that other children go to bed in the same way he does can help your child do the same.

This is a great time to write your baby his own book about sleep. This idea helped me successfully and gently wean my son David from breastfeeding when he was two and a half years old and can be used for other changes as well, such as sleeping through the night. Here's how.

Use poster board or very heavy paper. Your book should be large—8½″ × 11″ or bigger. Tape the pages together with heavy tape, but don't do so until you've created the entire book so you can easily replace any pages that you mess up.

Here I'll describe making two different types of books. Make either one, or even both!

Book One: My Sleep Book

Cut out many pictures of babies from magazines, advertisements, or the newspaper. Try to find pictures that pertain to sleep, such as a baby in a crib, or a baby getting a bath. Also cut out pictures of things that are part of your bedtime routine: picture books, a toothbrush, pajamas.

Use your pictures to create a book that demonstrates your exact bedtime routine, step by step. Write a story on the pages to go along with the pictures.

Read the book every night just before you begin your bedtime routine.

Book Two: The Personalized Growing-Up Book

Title your book *All About [insert Baby's name]*. It will depict the story of your baby's life, with the focus on sleeping (and feeding also if you use this idea to help wean Baby from the breast or bottle). You can also use this idea to wean Baby from the pacifier, or for that matter, to help Baby adjust to any major change in her life, such as introducing a new pregnancy, or dealing with divorce.

Gather pictures of your baby right from the time of birth. Start with a shot of her as a newborn, and progress through her life, finishing up with those pictures that feature actions and items in your bedtime routine. Pictures of Baby breastfeeding, drinking a bottle, using a pacifier, wearing pajamas, reading a book, lying in bed, and sleeping, are the most helpful. If possible, get a new roll of film and take photos of your baby during every step of your current bedtime routine—including several of him sleeping soundly. In one of the sleeping photos, have Mommy or Daddy in the background smiling and looking at Baby.

Each page will show a picture of your baby and explain what is happening. The book's ending will show your *goal* for your baby's sleeping, breastfeeding, bottle-feeding, or pacifier use. In other words, the book will portray the results you are aiming for.

This book will be very customized to your family. The following are excerpts from the book I created for David eight years ago. (As a lovely bonus, you'll have this book to cherish as your baby grows up. Excuse the tear stains as I write this portion.)

(Newborn photo: David nursing) David is a brand-new baby. His mommy and daddy love him very much. They are so happy he was born. David loves nursing and having Mommy's milk.

(Six-month photo: Angela giving him a bottle) David is getting bigger. He can crawl now. He loves to play with Angela and Vanessa. He still loves nursing and having Mommy's milk, and now he likes his bottle, too, especially when Angela or Vanessa help him have his bottle.

(Eleven-month photo: David walking) David is growing so much! He is starting to walk and throw a ball. He can have some real food too, and his favorite drink is chocolate milk. He still loves nursing and having Mommy's milk, and he likes his bottle, too.

Continue on in the book through your baby's life. Don't make the book so long that your little one will lose interest, because the ending is, after all, the real goal of the book. You know your own baby and how long of a book she enjoys.

The last section of the book will be your bedtime and sleep (or weaning) goals, outlined very clearly and specifically. Here is our ending:

(Second birthday photo) Happy birthday, David! You are a really big boy now. You can run and play and eat ice cream. You can go down a slide. You can take the dog for a walk. Big boys like David have a snack and then get in bed to go to sleep. They don't need Mommy's milk anymore—they just need lots of Mommy cuddles! Mommy and David can cuddle at bedtime, and then they both sleep all night long.

(Two-year-old photo: David sleeping) Mommy and David cuddle in the morning when the sun comes up. Everybody can hug and cuddle David in the morning. Congratulations, David! You are a big boy now.

(Pictures of everyone in the family with David)

Read this book every night. (Your baby may like it so much that she wants to read it during the day, too—and that's perfectly fine!) Talk about what you read. Help your little one do the things you talk about in the book.

After I made this book for David, we read and talked about it. He loved it! After a few monthss of reading and talking, David was weaned. The process was simple and loving, and we both felt good about it.

Make a Bedtime Poster

 This idea may help parents of babies who are more than twenty months old.

Most toddlers thrive on predictability and routine. They like it when the same things happen in the same way every day. This can be somewhat frustrating for you when your schedule happens to conflict with your toddler's regular naptime; you may be set on completing the day's errands, but your baby is ready to sleep and letting you know it with his fussy, whiny behavior. You can use your baby's desire for routine to your advantage when it comes to creating a healthy bedtime ritual.

We have already discussed the importance of a bedtime routine for all babies. Since your little one is older, you can involve him in the process. The most effective way to do this is to create a bedtime poster. Here's how:

- Get a large piece of poster board.
- Gather colorful markers or crayons.
- Follow the photo- or picture-gathering instructions from the previous section on making a bedtime book.
- Use the pictures and markers to create a fun, colorful poster that clearly demonstrates the steps to bedtime.
- Hang the poster on your child's bedroom door at his eye level.
- Have him help you follow the chart each night by asking him, "What's next?"
- Praise him for following the steps ("Good job!").

Here's a sample bedtime chart:

Joey's Bedtime Chart

1. Put on pajamas.
2. Have a snack.
3. Brush teeth.
4. Read three books.
5. Get drink of water.
6. Go potty.
7. Turn on Winnie-the-Pooh night-light.
8. Kisses, hugs, and back rub.
9. Joey goes to sleep.
10. Mommy and Daddy go to sleep.

For many toddlers, the chart alone will provide the consistency and routine that will ease them into bed each night.

If you have a child who wakes during the night crying for you, you can add your own preferred way to handle the issue to your chart. For example:

- When Jenna wakes up, she goes to her sleeping place in Mommy and Daddy's room—quiet as a mouse.

Or, here's another example:

- When Lily wakes up during the night when it's dark, she can go potty, get a drink of water, and hug her teddy bear. When Lily wakes up and it is light outside, she can climb quietly into bed with Mommy and Daddy.

This is a good time for you to think about exactly what you expect of your toddler and committing it to paper. Then help your little one to follow the steps—even during the night, "Remember your bedtime chart? This is what you need to do now."

If you have a little yo-yo who likes to get up after your routine, asking for a drink of water, a hug, or whatever, you can add this step to your chart to help eliminate this exasperating process:

- Alexander will get two Get-Out-of-Bed-Free cards. He may come out for potty, water, kisses, or hugs two times. When Alexander's tickets are gone, it is time to stay in bed and go to sleep.

These "cards" are simply pieces of paper that you create with your poster supplies. At the end of your routine, give your toddler the tickets. He has to give you a ticket each time he gets out of bed. Base the number of tickets on his current number of bed escapes, minus a few. That is, if he normally climbs out of bed five or six times, start with four tickets. After a week or so, change to three, and then two, and eventually, one. You may even want to let your child turn in any unused tickets in the morning for a small reward.

Always remember to praise your little one for following the bedtime routine.

Be Patient

This idea may help everyone.

One trait I noticed among many of my test mommies was an incredible eagerness to obtain results. That's absolutely under-standable! But patience, as the old saying goes, is a virtue. Some test mommies couldn't wait ten days to log their success, so they dutifully logged their babies' sleep patterns night after night after night, hoping to see change day by day, and getting frustrated if success was not evident. Getting this wired up over daily improvement will only keep you up at night (ironically). The log has a time and place. Complete one every ten days or so to see how far you have progressed, but none in between. Similarly, don't watch the clock all night. Simply follow your plan, and soon enough, both you and your baby will be sleeping.

5

Create Your Personal Sleep Plan

To move on to this step, you will have studied the ideas in Chapter 4 and noted those solutions that sound reasonable for your family. Now you can organize your plan, and get started on the path to better sleep!

Transfer the solutions you picked to the following section so that all your ideas will be summarized in one place. If you have a newborn, your form begins on page 160. If your baby is more than four months old, your form begins on page 162. Once you have created your personal plan you may want to copy the pages and post them in a prominent place, such as on your refrigerator or taped to your bathroom mirror. They will act as a daily reminder of the solutions you will be implementing. During the process, it will be helpful to refer back to the book when you need a refresher on any of the steps or ideas.

So, here you go! Use the forms that follow to create your own personal sleep plan.

My Personal Sleep Plan for My Newborn Baby

☐   I will learn more about babies and become confident in my beliefs.

•   The book(s) I will obtain and read now are: _____

_____

_____

_____

_____

_____

☐   I will put Baby to sleep often in the cradle, crib, or bed.

•   I'll reserve sleeping in my arms for special moments.

☐   I will remove my sleepy (instead of sleeping) baby from the nipple and help him go to sleep without something in his mouth.

•   I will avoid creating a sucking-to-sleep association.

☐   I will learn the difference between sleeping sounds and waking sounds.

•   I will let my sleeping baby sleep!

☐   I will make night sleeping different from daytime naps.

•   I will keep nighttime quiet, dark, and peaceful.

Taken from *The No-Cry Sleep Solution* by Elizabeth Pantley

☐ I will not let my baby take too long of a daytime nap.

• The longest I will let my baby nap is: _____

☐ I will watch for signs of tiredness.

• I will watch for: quieting down, losing interest, looking glazed, fussing, yawning; and I will put my baby to sleep when I see these signs.

☐ I will make my baby's sleep environment cozy and comfortable.

☐ I will make myself comfortable for night feedings and be accepting of this stage of my baby's life.

☐ I will fill my baby's tummy before sleep.

☐ I will enjoy restful feeding sessions during the day.

• This is what I should be doing. Relaxing and enjoying my new baby.

☐ I will simplify my life.

• My baby is my priority right now.

☐ I will have realistic expectations.

• My new baby will develop sleep maturity over the next few months. I can be patient until then.

Taken from *The No-Cry Sleep Solution* by Elizabeth Pantley

My Personal Sleep Plan for My Baby (Four Months to Two Years Old)

☐   I will get myself ready.

- My baby is old enough to sleep all night without my attention. He is biologically able to sleep all night, and many babies do. It will be good for my baby and it will be good for me. I am committed to doing things tonight that will help my baby sleep better. I don't want my baby to cry, so I am willing to be patient and make changes day by day. Soon we will both be sleeping all night long.

☐   I will get my baby ready.

- My baby is healthy.

- My baby is eating well during the day.

- My baby's sleeping place is inviting and comfortable.

☐   I will follow a bedtime routine.

- This is our nightly routine:

Approximate time	Activity

Taken from *The No-Cry Sleep Solution* by Elizabeth Pantley

☐ I will establish an early bedtime.

• My baby's new bedtime is: _____

• We begin our bedtime routine at: _____

☐ I will follow a flexible yet predictable daytime routine.

• This is a rough outline of our typical day (write in your planned awake time, naps, meal times, bedtime, and anything else that helps you organize your day):

Approximate time	Activity

☐ I will make sure that my baby takes regular naps.

• Times for my baby's naps are: _____

• I will watch my baby carefully for signs of tiredness: decreased activity, quieting down, losing interest, rubbing eyes, looking glazed, fussing, yawning; and I will put my baby down for a nap at those times.

• The ways I will encourage naps are: _____

Taken from *The No-Cry Sleep Solution* by Elizabeth Pantley

☐ I will help my baby learn how to fall asleep without help: (Idea One)

• I will spend daily quiet time letting my baby play in his bed.

☐ I will help my baby learn how to fall asleep without help: (Idea Two)

• I will encourage my baby to fall asleep for naps in these various places and ways: _____
_____
_____

☐ I will introduce a lovey.

• I will keep a lovey with us when we snuggle, and when I put my baby to bed.

☐ I will make night sleeping different from daytime naps.

• I will keep our nighttime quiet, dark, and peaceful.

☐ I will develop key words as a sleep cue.

• Our key words are: _____

☐ I will use music or sound as sleep cues.

• Our nighttime music/sounds are: _____
_____
_____

Taken from *The No-Cry Sleep Solution* by Elizabeth Pantley

☐ I will change my baby's sleep association.

- I'll use Pantley's Gentle Removal Plan as often as I can.

- Other things I will do: _____
_____
_____
_____

☐ I will help baby fall back to sleep while continuing to co-sleep.

- I won't respond too quickly; I'll wait for true "awake sounds."

- I'll shorten the duration of my nighttime help routine (nursing, rocking, or offering a bottle or pacifier).

- I'll use the gentle removal plan as often as I can.

- I'll scoot away from Baby after he falls asleep.

- I'll try to use key words and pat or massage Baby back to sleep.

☐ I will help Baby fall back to sleep and move him to his own bed.

- These are the things we will do: _____
_____
_____
_____

Taken from *The No-Cry Sleep Solution* by Elizabeth Pantley

☐ I will have my partner help Baby fall back to sleep.

• These are the things we will do: _____

_____

_____

• My helper will tend to Baby when he wakes, by doing these things: _____

_____

_____

• My helper will transfer Baby to me if Baby and/or helper gets upset, and then I will do these things: _____

_____

_____

☐ I will help my baby fall back to sleep step-by-step.

• This is my plan to shorten the duration and type of my nighttime help routine in these steps:

Phase One _____

_____

_____

Phase Two _____

_____

_____

Phase Three _____

_____

_____

Phase Four _____

_____

_____

Phase Five _____

_____

_____

Phase Six _____

_____

_____

☐ I will write a bedtime book and read it to my baby every night before bed.

☐ I will create a bedtime poster that shows our routine and follow it nightly.

☐ I will be patient, I will be consistent, and soon we will all be sleeping.

• I *will* have sleep success if I am persistent, consistent, and patient. I need to just relax, follow my plan, and do a log every ten days. After I do each log, I will analyze my success and make any revisions to my plan. Soon my baby and I will both be sleeping.

Taken from *The No-Cry Sleep Solution* by Elizabeth Pantley

6

Follow Your Plan for Ten Days

Now that you have created your own personal sleep plan, it's time to officially begin the process of helping your baby to sleep all night. How quickly you see sleep success will depend on how persistently you follow your plan. I strongly recommend that you make your baby's sleep a priority in your family for the next month or two. This means that you avoid going out during scheduled nap times or during your planned prebedtime routine and actual bedtime.

I know this can be a challenge. With three older children in our family, we sometimes seem to live on the road. Between school and after-school events, sports activities, birthday parties, and everything else, we're always on the go. When I was working on Coleton's sleep routines, I organized our days around his sleep times as much as possible. I made good use of car pools, called in favors, asked Grandma for help, and did anything else I could do so that Coleton would be home for his naps and bedtime routine. Once he began sleeping ten or more hours at night and taking a regular two-hour nap, I was able to relax and be more flexible. Once his sleep was consistent, we could extend his nap or bedtime by an hour or two, and he would just go right to sleep when we did get home and sleep later in the morning. Likewise, you won't be tied to your baby's nap and bedtime schedule forever, but the more consistent you can be right now, the sooner you will see sleep success.

Matthew, eleven months old, and Mike

What If You Can't Do It All?

You may start out motivated to follow your plan entirely, and then your efforts may be disrupted. Illness, vacations, visitors, and teething are just a few examples. You may find yourself giving up in the middle of the night, and berating yourself in the morning for abandoning your plan. It can be frustrating when these things happen. But hear me now: Even if you only follow part of your plan, and even if you can't be 100 percent consistent, you will still see sleep improvement. Even a few changes in your routines and habits can bring better sleep. And when things settle down around your house, you'll have a running start to really focus on your sleep plan and get your baby sleeping all night.

The Road to Success Is Really More Like a Dance

Most of you will find that attaining sleep success will not be a straight, easy road, even if you follow your plan perfectly. Instead, you will find that it's more like a dance: two steps forward, one step back, and even a few sidesteps in between.

I experienced this with Coleton. We'd had our very best night up until that point: He'd fallen asleep on his own and *stayed* asleep for seven hours. I was thrilled! A new level of success! But my party was short-lived. The very next night, he would not even *attempt* to go to sleep by himself; he nursed nearly constantly, and fussed in between sessions. Then he woke frequently, whining, "Mama, Mama" until I would nurse him again. I noticed this same pattern emerge with a number of my test mommies. I would get an E-mail shouting with joy, and a day or two later another message from the distressed mother asking, "What happened? She was up all night!"

Indeed, what happens? The variables are limitless. The baby gets sick, *you* get sick, he's teething, she missed a nap, he starts to crawl, she gets her vaccinations, you have company from out of town, or the moon is full. You may be able to pinpoint the reason, or maybe you'll be scratching your head wondering why your baby had such a rough night. And then the next night, your baby has the best night's sleep ever. Just more proof that babies are anything but predictable.

The good news is that, when you follow my sleep plan, this complicated dance does end up where you want to go. That's why the ten-day logs that I recommend are so important. When you have visible proof of successful improvements over a ten-day period, you can live with these annoying "sidesteps."

Maybe twenty, thirty, or even sixty days will pass before you achieve what you call a really good night's sleep—but in the big picture, a few months is nothing but a blink. That's another gift my four children have given me: perspective. I have a fourteen-year-old daughter. I know how quickly childhood passes. *Too* quickly, as I know you're sure to find. It seems as if I held my newborn Angela in my arms just yesterday, but before me now stands a lovely young woman in junior high school who borrows my clothes and my earrings, a person with her own strong opinions and fierce independence. (Oh, and did I mention that she sleeps through the night?)

So, here you go. Good luck with your sleep plan, and (soon) sweet dreams!

7

Do a Ten-Day Log

Now that you've followed your sleep plan for at least ten days, it's time to do another set of sleep logs, analyze your success, and make any necessary changes to your plan. In fact, you'll do this after every ten days that you follow your sleep plan (Chapters 9 and 10) up until you achieve the sleep results that you are comfortable with.

Ten is not a magical number—it's OK to log at whatever interval best suits you. I do suggest that you wait *at least* ten days between your logs, however, to give you and your baby ample time to adjust to your changes in routine. If you log more frequently than this, you may just frustrate yourself by focusing too hard on your desire for sleep and by looking for too much success too quickly (like hopping on the scale every day when you're on a diet).

Using the following forms, create your logs; be sure to read the instructions, and answer the questions. Read the information in the sections following each log and in the next chapter, which will help you analyze your logs.

Ten-Day Nap Log

Baby's Name: _____

Age: _____

Date: _____

How many days have you been following your plan? _____

Time baby fell asleep	How baby fell asleep	Where baby fell asleep	Where baby slept	How long?

1. Review Table 2.1 on page 48, or copy the information from your first log:
   How many naps should your baby be getting? _____
   How many naps is your baby getting *now*? _____
   How many hours should your baby be napping? _____
   How many hours is your baby napping *now*? _____
2. Do you have a formal nap routine? _____
3. Are you watching for sleepy signs and putting your baby down for a nap as soon as you notice he's tired? _____
4. Are your baby's naptimes/lengths consistent every day? _____

Ten-Day Prebedtime Routine Log

Baby's Name: _____

Age: _____

Date: _____

How many days have you been following your plan? _____

Key:
Activity: active, moderate, or calm
Noise: loud, moderate, or quiet
Light: bright, dim, or dark

Time	What we did	Activity level	Noise level	Light level

1. For the past ten days, approximately how many days did you follow your formal bedtime routine? _____
2. Is the hour prior to bedtime mostly peaceful, quiet, and dimly lit? _____
3. Does your bedtime routine help your baby wind down and prepare for sleep? _____
4. Is your nightly routine consistent, acting as a bedtime cue for your baby? _____
5. Is your bedtime routine relaxing and enjoyable for you? _____

Ten-Day Night-Waking Log

Baby's Name: _____

Age: _____

Date: _____

How many days have you been following your plan? _____

Time	How baby woke me up	How long awake; what we did	Time baby fell back to sleep	How baby fell back to sleep	How long of a sleep stretch since fell asleep

Asleep time: _____

Awake time: _____

Total number of awakenings: _____

Longest sleep span: _____

Total hours of sleep: _____

8

Analyze Your Success

It's time to think about what's happened since you began following your sleep plan. It's also the time to tweak your plan and make any changes that you've learned are necessary to help your baby sleep better. Because we can't sit down over a cup of coffee and talk about your baby (wouldn't that be nice!), I've created this chapter to help you figure out which parts of your plan are working, and which ones need to be changed. Start by using the information from your logs in Chapter 7 to complete the comparison chart that follows. Fill in the times from both logs and the amount of change:

	First log	Ten days	Amount of change
Number of naps			
Length of naps			
Bedtime: Asleep time			
Awake time			
Number of awakenings			
Longest sleep span			
Total hours of sleep			

Now take a few minutes to answer the following questions that will help you analyze your efforts. If you can, talk over the information with your spouse, your parenting partner, or another mother who is working on her own sleep plan. You may even want to search out a group of mothers and create a support group—either in person or by E-mail or bulletin board. The support of other parents who are going through the same things that you are right now can be very helpful and enlightening.

Evaluate Your Sleep Plan

During the past ten days, how closely did you follow your plan?

☐ I followed all parts of my plan exactly for all ten days.

☐ I followed some parts of my plan, but not everything.

☐ I started out great, but reverted back to my old habits.

☐ Plan? What plan? (Oops, better start over with Step One!)

Have you seen positive changes in at least one area (for example: a fifteen-minute increase in naptime or sleep span; an earlier bedtime; a reduction in the number of night wakings)? _____

What areas show the most change? _____

Why do you think that's true? (What have you done to influence this?) _____

What areas show the least change? _____

Why do you think that's true? (What have you done to influence this?) _____
_____
_____
_____

What have you learned about your baby's sleep habits over the past ten days? _____
_____
_____
_____
_____
_____
_____

What parts of your plan seem to be having the best influence on your baby's sleep? _____
_____
_____
_____

What changes do you think you now need to make? _____
_____
_____
_____

How are you going to make these changes? _____
_____
_____
_____
_____

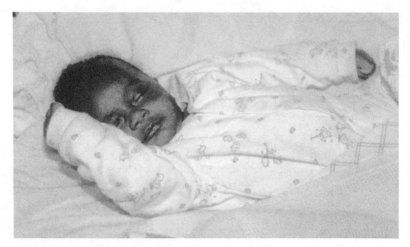

Reuel, one month old

The following sections are divided into three parts. Find the one that matches your level of success and read through the information. You may also want to read through the other sections for additional insight and ideas. Choose from these options:

If Your Baby Is Now Sleeping Through the Night (Five or More Consecutive Hours)

Congratulations! I'm truly thrilled that you have seen such great sleep success so quickly. I suspect that you have more energy and are feeling happier even though your sleep has improved for just a few days. It's amazing how a little sleep can have such a peaceful impact on your life, isn't it?

We need to address a few issues now that you've seen some success. First, this is only the beginning! Now that your baby can sleep five or more hours straight, you likely will see that span increasing little by little, night by night. You can help this along by continuing to follow your plan.

It's important to stick with your plan because your baby's sleep pattern is newly changed. If you revert back to your old ways, it's likely that your baby will, too; after all the work you've done, that would be very frustrating. Stay with your plan for a while (at least a few weeks) to make sure that the changes "stick."

Remember that babies' sleep patterns fluctuate. Don't be discouraged by an occasional night, or even a week, of sleep disruptions. All kinds of things can affect your baby's sleep: teething, sickness, vacations, visitors, vaccinations, or simply disruptions to your daily routine. Consistently stick to your plan, and over the next few months you will see your baby's sleep stabilize into a very comfortable pattern that is less and less affected by daily disruptions.

You may find that, now that your baby is sleeping longer spans, you are continuing to wake up in between these times. This can be the icing on the cake of frustration! If this is the case for you, you will find lots of ideas in Chapter 11.

If you are a breastfeeding mother, this sudden decrease in your baby's night wakings may cause you some discomfort because of engorgement. You can find solutions on pages 236–238.

Give yourself a pat on the back and give your baby a big hug. You did it!

If You Have Seen *Some* Success

Congratulations! Even if your baby isn't sleeping *all* night, I'm sure you're feeling much better about your baby's sleep—and yours! Take some time to think about what has happened since you've started using your sleep plan. Determine which ideas seem to be working best, and continue with those. Decide if any of the ideas aren't helping, and modify them or stop using them altogether. Once you have done this, proceed with your revised plan for ten more days; then, do another log and analysis.

Read though the next section to determine if there are any hidden issues standing in the way of more rapid sleep success.

If You Haven't Seen Any Positive Changes

I wish I could give you a hug. I know you are feeling very frustrated right now. But take heart. A number of my test mommies didn't see any changes at first, but once they evaluated what had occurred, reviewed the ideas, and modified their actions they began to see significant improvements. I'll try to help you figure out why the plan isn't working for you just yet.

Let's start by having you consider the possible issues that can block your success.

Have You Followed the Steps?

This book is set up very simply and lays out the approach step by step, in a specific and well-defined order. Is it possible that, in your desperation for sleep, you skipped important information? As an example, Chapter 2 explains how your baby sleeps; without benefit of this information, you won't understand the logic behind each idea. You may have made customized changes and unknowingly defeated the purpose of the suggestion. I suggest that you read over the first few sections of this book and begin anew. Don't get discouraged. Many parents have had to restart the plan, and they have gone on to fabulous sleep success, as you will, too.

If you realize that you've been skipping steps, go back to the beginning and fill in your gaps. Refine your plan, and let's get your baby sleeping!

Have You Chosen the Right Plan?

It is possible that you chose the wrong steps in your plan. Reread Chapter 2, and evaluate whether you've selected the most appropriate ideas for you and your baby. Once you've figured out which plan you should be following, renew your commitment.

Before now, you were living with your sleep disruptions without understanding them. Now that you've been thinking differently about your baby's sleep, you should be able to look clearly at what's preventing him from sleeping. Once you identify those issues, you can move forward with a successful sleep plan.

Are You Being Patient?

I know. You're tired. You want to sleep. Tonight.

Take a deep breath. You can do this. It won't take forever. If you focus on what's going wrong instead of what's going right, you'll just make yourself miserable, like this anxious test mommy did:

Mother-Speak

"It's amazing (and depressing) how consistent her waking-up pattern is—she's up every 1.75 hours. I find the sleeping process to be a lot more frustrating for me now that I am actually *trying* to fix it. It was easier on me mentally when I had just given up and accepted her constant night wakings."

Kelly, mother of eighteen-month-old Savannah

You may have heard about the amazing "two-day results" some-one had with a cry-it-out program, and you hoped to see the same kind of quick change in your baby—without the crying part, of course. Except that it's been ten whole days, and you've seen lit-tle or no improvement. Things may even seem worse than before.

Remember that back when we first met—in the Introduc-tion—I promised that I could get your baby to sleep through the night. I didn't promise a speedy miracle. Also, it is likely that your sleep issues will be more frustrating for you now that you are try-ing to solve the problem. Before today, it was easier to play ostrich—not willing to acknowledge the true frequency of your baby's night wakings, or how negatively they were affecting your life. Now that you're working on getting your baby to sleep longer, you'll be very focused on this part of your life and there-fore much more aware of your own lack of sleep.

I'm sure that your baby isn't so very different from all the oth-ers who have found success with this method. Take a quiet moment, review all the ideas, and analyze your sleep plan. I'm willing to bet that the next ten days will bring you closer to the results you are hoping for.

Have You Fully Committed to the Plan?

Sometimes parents begin the plan with a half-hearted attempt and hope to see miraculous changes. They review the sleep ideas,

Mother-Speak

"I realized that we were only partially following our plan. I guess we were hoping that changes would just magically happen. My husband and I talked today and agreed: no more casually following the ideas. Today we get serious."

Neela, mother of eighteen-month-old Abhishek

choose one or two that seem easy or quick, and then find themselves ten days later with no change in their baby's sleep pattern. Not until they *truly* commit to their plan do they see sleep success. Only you can determine if you have created a purposeful plan, given it honest effort, and followed it faithfully.

Have You Had Success, but You Don't Realize It?

You may be searching for absolute sleep success—those blissful eight straight hours without waking up, and you're missing the fact that your baby *is* sleeping better than before. Maybe you've logged two extra night wakings, and you're feeling disappointed. But wait! If your baby has slept more hours overall, then the number of wakings may not represent bad news at all! In other words, six wakings during a period of ten hours is a great improvement over five wakings during a period of eight hours. Or perhaps your baby's bedtime is an hour earlier than it was before. Or you're now taking only twenty minutes to put her to bed instead of an hour. Or each time she awakens at night she's only up for a few minutes, far less than she was keeping you up before. Take another look at your logs and compare them. Are you really having success, but you didn't see it at first?

Mother-Speak

"A few times I E-mailed my log to you feeling like a big failure, but then you would respond with congratulations over our improvement. Your comments would prompt me to look closer at our logs, and I would see that good things were definitely happening!"

Christine, mother of eighteen-month-old Emily

Have You Faced Setbacks or Unusual Situations?

If you have been struggling with your sleep plan because of teething, sickness, vacation, or any other disruption in your family routine, you will find your progress slower than it would have been had all these things not interfered with your baby's naps and nighttime sleep.

Mother-Speak

"When I first started with my plan, everything was going really well. But it seems that whenever I think we're making progress, things backfire. First the holidays hit, then he got a bad cold. Now he's teething, and it's waking him up every two or three hours again. I think he had a growth spurt in between, too. I told him I was going to sell him to the neighbors this morning, and we both laughed so hard."

Susan, mother of ten-month-old Luke

Such is the life of a parent! If you were ever bored before a baby entered your life, this new little person has erased the word from your vocabulary. Setbacks are an inevitable issue as you work your way through your sleep plan. Just keep moving forward. Despite all the interruptions, you *can* make progress. And when things settle down, you're likely to see that success is right around the corner.

Persistence and consistency are the keys. Do your best to stick to your plan despite the setbacks. Even if you can't manage every step, the ones that you do adhere to will create positive changes for you.

Typically, when life settles down, baby's sleep pattern will too. Here's a quote from the same mother a few weeks later:

> **Mother-Speak**
> "Finally his teeth have erupted, his congestion has ceased, and he is feeling much better. Here is last night's log—back to normal! This was Luke's first time sleeping more than six hours straight in about three weeks. I can't tell you how pleased I am. I guess the neighbors don't get him after all."
>
> **Susan, mother of ten-month-old Luke**

Are There Medical or Developmental Issues That Are Interfering with Baby's Sleep?

There may be more to your baby's inability to sleep than just habits and routines. You may be unaware of a medical or developmental issue that is impairing your baby's ability to sleep well. It's always wise to talk to your doctor if you have any concerns about your baby's health. Here are a few of the most common problems that keep babies up at night.

Teething

The process of teething is a common reason that babies have trouble falling and staying asleep. Think back to the last time you had a toothache, headache, sore back, or stiff neck. Discomforts can disrupt your ability to sleep. Babies can't tell us what the problem is; they can only cry or fuss. Often this behavior starts long before we see a tooth pop out, so it can be hard to tell that teething is responsible for your baby's fussiness.

Symptoms of Teething

Babies can begin the teething process as early as three months old. These symptoms typically accompany the teething process:

- Difficulty falling asleep or staying asleep
- Fussiness
- Drooling
- Runny nose
- Rash on the chin or around the mouth
- Biting
- Red cheeks
- Rejecting the breast or bottle
- Increased need to suck
- Swollen, discolored gums

Some parents report that a slight fever, diarrhea, vomiting, or diaper rash accompany teething, but because these symptoms also may signal an infection or virus, they should always be reported to your doctor.

How to Help Your Baby Feel Better

If you suspect that your baby is teething, the following interventions might relieve her discomfort so that she can relax enough to sleep:

- Give her a clean, cool washcloth to chew on.
- Let her chew on a teething ring that is either room temperature or chilled in the refrigerator (not frozen).
- Frequently and gently pat her chin dry.
- Offer a sip of cold water.
- Rub her gums with a clean, wet finger.
- Use a specially made baby toothbrush to clean the gums.
- Dab petroleum jelly or a gentle salve on her chin in the drool area.
- Breastfeed often, for comfort as well as nutrition.

The teething pain relief ointments that are available over the counter can be quite potent (put a dab on your lip and you'll notice a tingly, numbing feeling). So, use these sparingly and only with an OK from your doctor.

Separation Anxiety

As your baby gets older, she will begin to become aware of her "separateness" from you. She lives in the present, and has a limited sense of time and memory; so when you leave her, she wonders where you go and worries that you may not come back. This is called separation anxiety. According to Dr. Avi Sadeh, in *Sleeping Like a Baby* (Yale University Press, 2001):

> Separation anxiety is one of the main causes of sleep disorders in early childhood.
>
> The rise in the frequency of sleeping disorders during the first year of life may be linked to the appearance of the separation anxiety that is a normal developmental occurrence at this age.
>
> A change such as the mother's return to work after maternity leave, a new caretaker, the transition to day care, or any change that signifies separation and a new adaptation is frequently expressed immediately in the form of a significant sleep disorder.

Dr. Sadeh explains that even a temporary separation, such as the mother going to the hospital to give birth to a new sibling or leaving for an overnight event, can have a powerful impact on a baby's sleep pattern. His research showed that even after the separation, babies woke up more often, cried more often, and spent less time sleeping in general.

Many parents find that as their baby enters the developmental stages of crawling and walking, separation anxiety peaks. This is because your baby learns that she can move away from you— and you from her.

Help for Separation Anxiety

When separation anxiety hits, let her know that you, or some-one who cares for her, is always nearby. Here are some ways to send this message to your little one:

- Increase your daytime nurturing by giving Baby more hugs and cuddles.
- Follow a peaceful, consistent routine in the hour before bedtime.
- Keep a large photo of Mommy and Daddy near your baby's bedside.
- When Baby is awake, don't sneak away when she's not look-ing. Always say good-bye or good night on your way out.
- Show confidence and joy when you leave your baby, not insecurity or fear. Respond quickly to Baby's nighttime calls or cries, even if it's just to say, "I'm here and everything's OK."
- Help your child develop an attachment to a lovey (see pages 117–119) so that she'll have something to hug when you're away.
- During the day, periodically step away from your baby and go into another room while singing or whistling, so that your baby knows that while she can't see you, you are still there.

Developmental Milestones and Growth Spurts

Commonly, a baby who is learning a new developmental skill awakens in the night with a sudden need to practice it. This is usually a short-lived sleep disruption and tends to go away as soon as the new skill is mastered.

Similarly, your baby might suddenly be eating more, sleeping less, and growing out of his clothes almost before the price tags

**Mother-Speak

"I've noticed with my babies that the first few days after they learn to do something new, like crawling or pulling up to standing, they sleep restlessly. When they wake up in the middle of the night, they immediately want to do their new 'trick.' If I weren't so tired, it would be funny to see Thomas or Rebecca go straight from sleeping into crawling or standing! After a while, they seem to get used to their new abilities, and then they sleep better."

Alice, mother of six-month-old twins Rebecca and Thomas

are cut off. This is a growth spurt, and your baby is doing some serious growing—day and night.

The key to handling these types of night wakings is to help your baby lie back down and get resettled with a minimum amount of time and fuss involved. Often using your key words and gentle patting or rubbing will help, because often your baby won't even be fully awake.

Mother-Speak

"It never occurred to me that Kyra's new skills could be making her restless at night. Every morning for the past two weeks I've found her standing up in her crib in the wee hours. Now that you mention this, I realized that she has been pulling herself up to stand on anything she can during the day for the same two weeks!"

Leesa, mother of nine-month-old Kyra

General Illness and Discomfort: Colds, Sniffles, Fever, and Immunizations

Just like an adult, a baby who does not feel well will not sleep well. However, unlike an adult, he doesn't know why he feels bad, nor does he know how to help himself feel better. When your baby isn't feeling well, do what you can to make him comfortable. Back off a bit on your sleep plan for a few days.

Here are some suggestions that might help your baby feel better:

- **Let your baby rest.** Put off running errands, having visitors, or doing anything else that disrupts your baby's quiet recovery time. This also helps you stay calm and peaceful so that you can help your baby to recover.
- **Give lots of fluids.** No matter what the illness, your baby will feel better if he is well hydrated. If you are breastfeeding, nurse frequently. If your baby drinks from a cup or bottle, provide lots of breast milk, formula, juice, and water. For older babies, add popsicles, soup, and ice chips.
- **Pamper and cuddle.** You may have to put everything else on hold for a few days. The more you try to accomplish when your baby is sick, the fussier she will be.
- **Clear your baby's nose so that he can breathe easily.** Do this by using saline nasal spray mist (ask your pharmacist for a recommendation) followed by suction with a nasal aspirator made especially for babies.
- **Keep the air moist.** During sleep times, use a humidifier or vaporizer with clean distilled water.
- **Encourage as much sleep as possible.** Do those things that work best to help your baby nap and sleep well.
- **Talk to a doctor anytime your baby is sick.** Someone at your pediatrician's office or your local hospital is always available to give you advice on how to treat your baby's illness.

Gas and Colic

All babies have gas, but some babies struggle more with releasing it from their systems. Your baby may swallow air when feeding or crying, which can result in an uncomfortably full feeling, gas, or even stomach pains.

You may have heard the term colic applied to any baby who cries a lot. Not all crying babies have colic, however—but all colicky babies cry. Though researchers are still unsure of its exact cause, most believe that colic is related to the immaturity of a baby's digestive system. Some also think that a baby's immature nervous system and inability to handle the constant sensory stimulation that surrounds her might cause a breakdown by the end of the day. Whatever the reason, it's among the most exasperating conditions new parents face. Symptoms include:

- A regular period of inconsolable crying, typically late in the day
- Crying bouts that last one to three hours or more
- Age range of three weeks to four months old
- Baby is healthy and happy at all other times of the day

It's Not Your Fault

Because colic occurs when a baby is so young, new parents often feel that they are doing something wrong to create the situation. Their vulnerability and lack of experience puts them in the position of questioning their own ability to care for their baby. Because you are a parent who doesn't believe in letting a baby cry to sleep, I know that hearing your baby cry with colic is especially painful for you, as it was for me when colic struck our home.

Although I've handled all of my babies similarly, only one of my four had colic. It was a dreadful experience, but I learned a lot about myself and my baby through the process. Please allow my personal experience with colic, as well as my research and discussions with other parents, to put your mind at ease. *It's not your fault.* Any baby can have colic. The only good thing about colic is that, by the time your baby is three to four months old, it will magically disappear and become just a blip in your memory.

Help with Colic

There is no simple, effective treatment for colic. By using their experience, parents and professionals are able to offer suggestions that may help your baby though this time period. Experiment with everything on this list until you find the interventions that help your baby best. Keep in mind that there is no magical cure, and nothing you do will completely eliminate colic until your baby's system is matured and able to settle on its own. Until then, do what you can to help calm your baby and yourself.

- If breastfeeding, feed on demand as often as your baby needs to stay calm.
- If breastfeeding, avoid eating foods that may cause gas in your baby, such as dairy, caffeine, cabbage, broccoli, and other gassy vegetables.
- If bottle-feeding, offer frequent smaller meals; experiment with different formulas.
- If bottle-feeding, try different types of bottles and nipples that prevent air from entering your baby as he drinks.
- Hold your baby in a more upright position for feeding and directly afterward.
- Offer meals in a quiet setting.
- If Baby likes a pacifier, offer her one.
- Burp Baby more often.
- Invest in a baby sling or carrier, and use it during colicky periods.
- Bring your stroller in the house and use it to walk baby around.

- Give Baby a warm bath.
- Place a warm towel or wrap a warm water bottle and place it on Baby's tummy (taking caution that the temperature is warm but not hot).
- Hold Baby in a curled position, with legs curled up toward belly.
- Massage Baby's tummy.
- Swaddle the baby in a warm blanket and walk her in the stroller.
- Lay Baby tummy down across your lap and massage or pat her back.
- Hold Baby in a rocking chair, or put him in a swing.
- Walk with Baby in a quiet, dark room.
- Lie on your back and lay Baby on top of you, tummy down, while massaging his back. (Transfer Baby to his bed when he is asleep.)
- Take Baby for a ride in the car.
- Play soothing music or turn on white noise.
- Ask your doctor about special medications available for colic and gas.

Tips for Parents with a Colicky Baby

Use the following suggestions to help you cope with the stress of having a colicky baby. Remember that if you're taking care of yourself and simplifying your life, you'll be available to offer comfort to your baby during her unhappy periods.

- Plan outings for the times of day when Baby is happy.
- Know that your baby *will* cry during his colicky time and while you can do things to make your baby more comfortable, nothing you can do will *totally* stop the crying.
- Take advantage of another person's offer to take a turn with the baby, even if it's just so that you can take a quiet bath or shower.

- Keep in mind that this is only a temporary condition; it will pass.
- Try lots of different things until you discover what works best.
- Avoid keeping a long to-do list right now; only do what's most important.
- Talk to other parents of colicky babies so you can share ideas and comfort each other.
- If the crying is getting to you and making you tense or angry, put your baby in her crib, or give her to someone else to hold for a while so that you don't accidentally shake or harm your baby.
- Know that babies do not suffer long-term harm from having colic.

When Should the Doctor Be Called?

Anytime you are concerned about your baby, put in a call to the doctor. In the case of colic, you should definitely make that call if you notice any of the following:

- The crying is accompanied by vomiting
- Your baby is not gaining weight
- The colic lasts longer than four months
- Your baby seems to be in pain
- Your baby doesn't want to be held or handled
- The crying spree isn't limited to one bout in the evening
- There are no regular bowel movements or wet diapers
- You notice other problems that don't appear on the previous list of symptoms

Ear Infections

If your baby has been very fussy, is waking up more than usual, wakes up crying as if he's in pain, or pulls at his ears, your baby may have an ear infection. Ear infections are very common in babies because their ear tubes are short, wide, and horizontal, giving bacteria from the nose and throat a fast, easy path to the ears. As babies get older and their ear tubes mature, they will no longer be so susceptible to ear infections. In the meantime, an untreated ear infection will prevent your baby from sleeping well.

Causes and Symptoms of Ear Infections

Ear infections occur when bacteria and fluid build up in the inner ear, often after a cold, sinus infection, or other respiratory illness. The fluids get trapped in the ear, causing a throbbing pain. Ear infections are not contagious, although the illnesses that typically precede them are.

Your baby may exhibit all of these, some of these, or even none of the symptoms. It's always important to see your pediatrician if you even suspect an ear infection. A gut feeling that something isn't quite right is justification enough for a call or a visit to the doctor. Listen to your instincts.

These symptoms *might* indicate an ear infection:

- A sudden change in temperament: more fussiness, crying, and clinginess
- An increase in night waking (as if you need this!)
- Waking up crying as if in pain
- Fever
- Diarrhea
- Reduced appetite or difficulty swallowing (Baby may pull away from the breast or bottle and cry even when hungry.)
- Runny nose that continues after a cold
- Drainage from the ear
- Fussiness when lying down that goes away when baby is upright

These symptoms almost always indicate an ear infection:

- Frequent pulling, grabbing, or batting at the ears that is not done playfully, but rather with apparent discomfort
- Green, yellow, or white fluid draining from the ear
- An unpleasant odor emanating from the ear
- Signs of difficulty hearing

What to Do About an Ear Infection

If your baby is exhibiting any symptoms and you suspect an ear infection, make an appointment with your doctor right away. Hearing a doctor say, "His ears look fine, he's just teething" is far better than letting your baby (and you) suffer through an untreated infection. Seeing your doctor is also important because an untreated ear infection can lead to speech difficulties, hearing loss, meningitis, or other complications.

Your doctor may suggest some of the following if your baby does have an ear infection (but don't try to solve this problem on your own without a doctor's direction):

- Give a pain reliever, such as acetaminophen (Tylenol) or ibuprofen. (Do not give your baby aspirin unless a doctor tells you to.)
- Keep Baby's head elevated for sleep. You can do this by raising one end of her mattress (try taping tuna cans under one end or some of the ideas on page 201), putting her to sleep in a stroller or car seat, or letting her fall asleep in your arms or in a sling.
- Place a warm compress over the affected ear.
- Keep the ears dry and out of water.
- Offer plenty of liquids.
- Use prescribed ear drops.
- Administer prescribed antibiotics.
- Keep your baby home from day care or baby-sitters.

Reduce the Chance of Ear Infections

Any baby can get an ear infection, but you can take a few measures to reduce the likelihood:

- **Prevent the colds and flu that introduce the bacteria into your child's system.** Wash your baby's and your hands frequently. Encourage anyone who holds your baby to wash her hands first, particularly if she or anyone in her family has a cold. Keep your baby away from anyone who is obviously sick with a cold or flu.
- **Keep your baby away from cigarette smoke.** Just one afternoon spent with secondhand smoke can increase your baby's chances of developing an ear infection.
- **Breastfeed your baby for a minimum of six months.** The antibodies and immune system boosters in breast milk discourage bacterial growth. In addition, the way your baby drinks from the breast (vigorous sucking and frequent swallowing) helps prevent milk from flowing into the ears. Breastfed babies are far less prone to ear infections than those who are bottlefed.
- **Never prop a bottle for your baby, or leave your baby to sleep with a bottle.** This can cause milk to pool in the mouth and seep into the ear canals. (And it may also cause decay in your baby's teeth.)

Reflux (Gastroesophageal Reflux—GER)

Gastroesophageal refers to the stomach and esophagus. *Reflux* means to return or flow back. Gastroesophageal reflux is when the stomach's contents flow back up into the esophagus. A baby with reflux suffers from heartburn-like stomach pains, which will tend to be most uncomfortable when she is lying down for sleep. This makes it hard for her to fall and stay asleep. Reflux is most often caused by an immature digestive system, and almost all babies with reflux will outgrow the problem.

The following are the most common symptoms of reflux:

- Spitting up or vomiting frequently
- Difficulty feeding or fighting feeding even when hungry
- Guzzling or frantic swallowing
- Crying that appears to be a sign of pain
- Waking in the night with a burst of crying
- Fussiness and crying after eating
- Increase in fussing or crying when lying on his back
- Decrease in fussiness when held upright or when lying on stomach
- Frequent colds or recurrent coughing
- Spitting up when straining to have a bowel movement
- Frequent hiccups
- Sinus and nasal congestion
- Losing weight

If your baby shows some of these symptoms, you should talk to your doctor about the possibility of reflux. Once your doctor has confirmed your suspicion, he may suggest some of these remedies:

- Offer frequent, small meals as opposed to fewer, larger feedings.
- Hold your baby upright for thirty to sixty minutes after feeding.
- Have a supervised period of tummy-down time with baby on a thirty-degree angle after feeding. Remember that most babies should sleep on their backs—according to the American Academy of Pediatrics, even those babies with reflux. If your baby has severe reflux, talk to your doctor about a possible alternative for your baby.

- Avoid putting baby in a sitting position that could result in her becoming slumped over (such as in an infant seat) directly after eating.
- Elevate the head of your baby's bed by using a higher setting on the crib mattress, by placing something stable under the legs of the bed or crib, or by placing a block of wood or books under the mattress.
- For a bottle-fed baby, switch to a different brand of formula, or try a thicker variety. Experiment with different bottle types and nipple styles to reduce excess air.
- For a breastfed baby, give frequent, smaller feedings. If your baby is ready for solid food, add a small serving of rice cereal after nursing.
- Avoid putting the baby in clothing that is tight around the belly.
- Avoid letting your baby cry for any length of time, as crying can make reflux worse. Carry your baby as much as possible to decrease crying.
- Avoid any exposure to secondhand smoke.

If reflux is severe, talk to your doctor about medical remedies, such as using a children's antacid.

Allergies and Asthma

If a baby has a condition that affects his breathing, it usually affects his sleeping too. Parents may be struggling with a baby who wakes frequently at night and they might not be aware that the cause is allergies or asthma.

Symptoms of Allergies and Asthma

Sometimes it's hard to tell the difference between a common cold and a more serious condition. Here are the signs of allergies and asthma to look for:

- Runny nose
- Coughing, especially at night
- Sniffling
- Sneezing
- Stuffy nose, especially upon waking
- Itchy eyes, ears, or nose
- Watery eyes
- Sore throat
- Difficulty breathing
- Skin rash
- Diarrhea
- Cold symptoms that last more than two weeks
- Persistent, chronic ear infections
- An increase in these symptoms after contact with animals or being outside near plants and flowers

Only a doctor can tell if your child truly has allergies or asthma, because many of the symptoms resemble those we normally attribute to a cold, respiratory congestion, or other normal childhood conditions, like teething. If you suspect that your child may have either condition, it's important to talk to your doctor about your concerns.

Nightmares, Night Terrors, and Sleepwalking or Talking

Older babies may have their sleep interrupted by a variety of common sleep disturbances. Your baby may occasionally wake up crying or talking in her sleep, or she may move around, sit up, or even crawl or walk in her sleep. The majority of these incidents are infrequent and short-lived.

The best option for parents in these situations is to calm your baby as best you can and help her to go back to sleep. If any sleep disturbance persists, talk to your doctor about your concerns.

Snoring and Sleep Apnea

If your baby is a very restless, noisy sleeper; breathes through his mouth; and snores or snorts loudly, he may be suffering from sleep apnea. *Apnea* means "absence of breath." The most disturbing symptom of this sleep disorder is that the sleeper actually stops breathing for up to thirty seconds, occasionally longer. This is very frightening for a parent to witness and should be taken very seriously, but in general, it is not life threatening and can be treated. Up to 10 percent of children have significant sleep apnea. The main causes include a narrow throat or airway, enlarged tonsils or lymph nodes, obesity, and facial abnormalities. Additional symptoms that may appear in older children are daytime sleepiness, nightmares, bed-wetting, sleep terrors, sleepwalking, sweating profusely while asleep, and morning headaches.

Not every child who snores has sleep apnea. However, if snoring is loud or is combined with the other symptoms, apnea could be the problem. Conversely, not all children with narrow airways, enlarged tonsils, or excess weight have sleep apnea.

Untreated apnea can cause heart problems and high blood pressure, in addition to significant sleep deprivation. Studies have been unable to link sleep apnea to the incidence of SIDS.

What Is the Cure?

The most common remedy for childhood sleep apnea is removal or reduction of the tonsils or adenoids. Other typical treatments are enlarging the air passage, holding the passage open during sleep, or (when the condition is caused by obesity) weight loss.

Checking Baby for Sleep Apnea

All parents should check their sleeping babies from time to time. In a quiet room, your baby's breathing should be barely audible; it should be through his nose and appear effortless and regular.

(This does not hold true if your baby has a cold or stuffy nose, although it's important to know that children with sleep apnea often have exaggerated symptoms when they have colds.)

If your baby's breathing during sleep is through his mouth, loud, accompanied by snoring or wheezing, or if he appears to be struggling to breathe, talk to your pediatrician; an ear, nose, and throat specialist; or a sleep disorders clinic about the possibility of sleep apnea. If your baby is a newborn, these signs can be extremely serious and should be reported immediately.

Moving Forward with Your Sleep Plan

Now that you've analyzed your baby's current sleep situation and uncovered any possible problems, it's the time to tweak your plan. Reread the ideas section, polish up your plan, and follow it for ten more days. At that time, you'll do another log, and, if you do your work, I know that you'll be sleeping like a baby—*your* baby, the one who sleeps all night long.

9

Follow Your Plan for Ten More Days

At this point in your sleep plan, it's important that you've followed the steps in Chapters 7 and 8. Those sections will help you figure out how to best use your plan for the next ten days. You may have discovered that you need to change a few of the parts of your plan. You may have realized that your baby's sleep habits are different from what you first suspected, and you need to add or even remove a few of your original ideas. Or, you may have determined that your plan is the right one, and you just need to recommit to another ten days.

Now that you've had some time to live with these new ideas you'll begin to understand more of what you've read and how to apply the concepts. You might have had a few "aha!" moments, when something your baby does clicks with something you've read, and you suddenly have a deeper understanding of the rationale behind the solutions.

Every Baby Is Different; Every Family Is Different

I'm always a bit suspicious of those charts about baby development and milestones that tell you exactly what to expect at every week of age. Babies are as different from one another as we adults

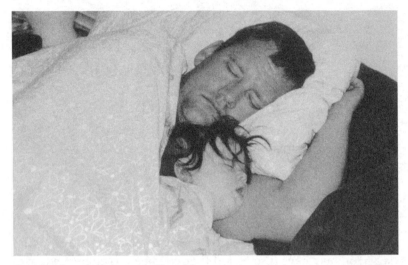

Jim and Lauren, nine months old

are different from each other, and to assume that all babies do the exact same things at the exact same time is simply not reasonable. As the mother of four children, I *know* that babies develop on extremely different time lines. My children demonstrated the uniqueness of their own development as they all passed the major milestones at very different times. Vanessa was only eighteen months old when she used her first sentence, "Cookie Mommy please," while Angela waited to begin talking in full sentences until she was nearly two and a half. David walked at ten months, and ran soon after that, while Coleton was content to crawl and be carried until he was sixteen months old. As you already know, Angela didn't sleep through the night until she was two, while Vanessa managed that feat all on her own at six weeks of age. What's most interesting about these comparisons is that now, at ages two, ten, twelve, and fourteen all of my children talk and walk perfectly, and they all sleep through the night. My point here is that babies are unique. There are things that you can do to help your baby sleep *better*, but the time when your little one sleeps all night, every night is also affected by his individual temperament and physiology. Therefore, it's best if you don't compare your baby's sleep habits to other babies, but rather to his own schedule week by week. *Your* success will be found by noting improvements in your individual baby's patterns as you work through your sleep plan.

How Long Is This Going to Take?

Patience, patience. We are dealing with a real live little human being here, not a computer that can be programmed. While it would be pure brilliance if I could invent a one-day-no-cry-sleep-solution, I don't harbor any fantasies that such a plan exists. I suggest that you celebrate every piece of success along your way. Taking a longer nap now? Great! Falling asleep quicker? Wonderful! Sleeping longer stretches at night? Hallelujah! If you can honestly appreciate each little victory along the way you'll feel better about this whole sleep issue. You *are* on the path to all-night sleep. It will happen. Now is the time to recommit to your plan for another ten days. Good luck as you continue on your journey to all-night sleep!

"I've Tried Everything! Nothing Works! Help!"

The ideas in this section are intended for anyone at the end of the rope or anyone who is ready to give up and let the baby cry it out.

For so many different reasons, not every test mommy I worked with had fabulous, immediate success. A few parents struggled for weeks until they felt it was completely hopeless. Some were able to reevaluate what was happening, make some plan adjustments, and go on to success. Others struggled still, like these two families:

"I have nothing good to report. I began two logs for you and failed to complete both. The first one, I got only as far as 10:41 P.M. It was unbelievable! She was up so many times I just couldn't keep up. She slept in our bed and kept waking up. It is crazy. It is enough already. We are beyond exhausted! I don't want to be the one test mommy who fails the program, but it looks like it is headed in that direction. Every day, my husband and I talk about letting her cry it out. We even tried to let her cry for one minute and even got up to two minutes, but neither one of us could go beyond that, so even though we threaten to do it, I don't think that letting her cry herself to sleep is an option. We don't know what to do."

"I cannot cope anymore. I feel like I am totally losing it. Once again, I have gone from bed to bed all night long. I can hardly function. He is awake now and he's been awake nursing on and off since 4 A.M. It's now after six, and every time I pop him off he cries like I am hurting him. It's just ridiculous, and I am beginning to hate nursing! This is horrible. I have been crying. My friends are no help at all. They say, 'See, I told you so. You should never have spoiled him. You should just let him cry, he'll go to sleep.' I know that they're wrong and that I am doing the right things with my baby, but I cannot take this 'no sleeping' much longer."

If you are at this point in *your* life, I'm going to give you three ideas that are drastically different from anything else I have suggested. You are obviously at a dangerous level of extreme emotions, and you don't want to accidentally hurt your baby in the night by shaking or hitting her. These things can happen when you get to this point. (Even the most connected and loving parent can get pushed to anger by severe sleep deprivation.) You also don't want to begin to resent your baby or find your sleeplessness interfering with what should be joyful days with your baby.

As long as your baby is more than four months old, you can use any of the following three ideas. Take a day and think about them. Talk the ideas over with your husband, or a friend you can trust. Take a deep breath. (If your baby is younger than four months old, please read the section about newborns that begins on page 64.)

Idea Number One: Take a Break

For the next week, do not fight the night wakings at all. Do whatever works to get your baby back to sleep fastest. Get rid of your bedroom clock, or at least turn it around so that you can't see it. Go to bed as early as possible, and stay in bed as late as you can in the morning. Prioritize your life, and don't do anything that can wait a week to get done. Take naps when and if you can. Call this your "I'll do anything just to get some sleep" week. Do this for a week, or even two, as a breather and then go back to the ideas with a fresh outlook. Or, if it seems to work for you, do it for a month, and see if your baby will outgrow her night waking on her own. I'll be honest and say that it's unlikely to happen that way. But after filling your sleep tank, and paying off some of your mounting sleep debt, you'll feel better and be much more able to approach a sleep plan.

During this time, read Chapter 8, especially the section beginning on page 182. The information in this section may be able to help you figure out what problems are preventing you from having sleep success.

Idea Number Two: Get Serious

Continue to follow the steps in this book with one major change. Get serious! No more "maybes," "kind-ofs," "really shoulds," or "next times." Take some quiet time to reread the first parts of this book, focus, and concentrate. Create a plan for yourself based on what you learn about sleep and what you know about yourself and your baby. Have confidence in the program because it can work for you. Follow every idea religiously.

If your baby spends all or part of the night in bed with you, and continues to wake many times during the night, you may have to move her to her crib in order to gain longer sleep stretches. This will require that you get up and down for a few days but should end up with your baby sleeping longer. You will find ways to do this beginning on page 137. Once she's sleeping soundly and consistently, you always have the option of bringing her back to your bed if you wish.

Many of the parents who reached the point of utter frustration discovered that they were only following the suggestions partway—hoping success would happen anyway. Following the suggestions half-heartedly will only bring you minor success, if any at all.

Please reread the Introduction, and review the entire section of solutions found in Chapter 4. Modify your plan as necessary and follow it exactly, and your baby will sleep. Now is a good time to read Chapter 12 for some encouragement.

The majority of parents who follow my plan faithfully see outstanding results in thirty days or less. You can do it too.

Idea Number Three: A Temperate Alternative to Letting Baby Cry It Out

If you are ready to give up, if you are geared up to toss this book and all my ideas out the window and just let your baby cry it out, then this section is written for you.

Dr. Sears calls the place where you are "the danger zone," and he warns that if your baby's nighttime routine is making you angry, and making you resent your baby, something must change. Again, I'm including the following suggestion because you are at your wit's end. It may work beautifully, or it may just upset you more. Think about it first, before you make your decision to try it. If at any point you feel that it's making things worse instead of better, go immediately to Idea Number One and take a week to reevaluate what's happening.

This suggestion is more appropriate if your baby is more than one year of age. But, if you have a younger baby (older than four months), and you are on the verge of putting your baby in a crib and earplugs in your ears, then this is a better alternative. Here are the steps to a temperate alternative to cry it out.

1. Give your baby extra one-on-one time during the day (especially morning and before bedtime). Increase the amount of time during the day that you cuddle, hold, and carry your baby.

2. Teach your baby the difference between light and dark. (Take her in a bathroom and play a game—lights out: dark! Lights on: light! Read books about opposites. Morning and evening, comment on the time of day as you look out the window.)

3. At bedtime, explain your expectations clearly. For example, you might tell her, "We nurse (or have a bottle) when it's light. We sleep when it's dark." Look for some board books about babies and sleep. Or write your own book (see pages 151–154). Read these books to your baby as part of your bedtime routine.

4. When your baby wakes up during the night, repeat your expectations. For example you would say, "Shhhh. Night night. We nurse in the light. We sleep in the dark. It's dark now. We sleep." Pat her or rub her and tell her it's time to go to sleep.

5. She will cry. She may cry a lot. She may get really upset. Be prepared for this and tell yourself, "She's going to be OK. I am only going to do this for [you fill in how many] nights." (Choose how many nights you are willing to do this.)

6. If you find you can't let her cry in her crib, even with you standing at her bedside, you can then hold her, rock her, hum to her, rub her back, put your cheek against hers, anything that helps her or you. (If your husband or another of your baby's caregivers can handle this part, it's often much easier on both Baby and Mommy.)

7. If your baby does not depend on nursing or a bottle, but wakes you repeatedly to be held or rocked, you can use this same idea. Except, keep your baby in his crib, and lean over to pat, rub, or otherwise soothe your baby while keeping him in his crib. (One mother tried this and actually fell asleep on the floor with her hand through the crib slats, patting her baby's bottom!)

8. Whisper words of comfort (these are mainly to keep you calm, and can also help your baby know that you are there). "This will all be over in a couple days. I love you. It's OK. Mommy's here. Time to sleep."

9. At any point that either you or your baby are too upset, go ahead and nurse, give her a bottle, or resort to whatever method calms her down and helps her go back to sleep. By this point your baby will be very tired; she will fall asleep quickly and stay asleep longer. There is no reason to push yourself or your baby to the limit. Just try again with the next night waking, or tomorrow night.

10. You may want to choose a time when you stop the process for the night. For example, "I'm going to do this until 3:00 A.M. After that I'm going to just bring her to bed so we can both get some sleep."

11. I know that we both believe that any crying is bad. But if Mommy is at the end of her rope, with no more patience for gradual adjustments, or if Daddy is threatening to move to a motel, it may be the last resort. You have been a very attached mommy, and your baby has been nurtured and loved. Certainly, being well rested and peaceful is important for both of you. Martha and Williams Sears in *The Breastfeeding Book* declare, "Crying and fussing in the arms of a loving parent is not the same as crying it out." So if you feel you must resort to this process, don't beat yourself up over it. Just get through it as quickly as possible, and give your baby lots of daytime love and snuggles.

12. Remember, at any time, even in the middle of the night, it's perfectly OK for you to give up this idea and use Idea Number One on page 209.

10

Complete a Log, Analyze Your Success, and Revise Your Plan as Necessary Every Ten Days

Now that you've followed your sleep plan for at least a second set of ten days, it's time to do another set of sleep logs, analyze your success, and make any necessary changes to your plan. You will also use the information in this chapter after every ten days that you follow your sleep plan until you feel satisfied with how your baby is sleeping.

Using these forms, create your new logs, and again, be sure to read the instructions that follow them. Photocopy the forms to make sure that you have enough to take you through to your ultimate and final sleep success, or create your own in a notebook.

Review the information in Chapter 8 as you move through this process.

Keep This Book Handy

Even after your baby sleeps through every night, and naps like a dream, it's highly possible that you'll still experience setbacks over the next few years. All of the issues that we discussed in

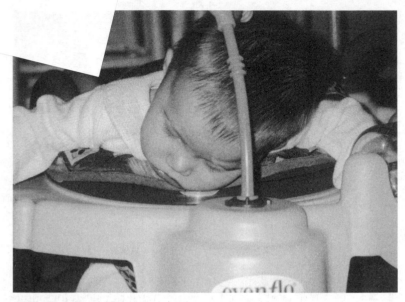

Coby, five months old

Chapter 8 (such as ear infections, teething, and vacations) are likely to disrupt even the best sleeper's schedule. Don't fret too much about this normal occurrence. Just dig out this book and follow your plan for a week or two to get your baby back on track.

Use the logs and the evaluations on the following pages every ten days until you reach your ultimate sleep success, and then use them at any time in the future when your baby's sleep needs an adjustment.

Ten-Day Nap Log

Baby's Name: _____

Age: _____

Date: _____

How many days have you been following your plan? _____

Time baby fell asleep	How baby fell asleep	Where baby fell asleep	Where baby slept	How long?

1. Review Table 2.1 on page 48, or copy the information from your first log:
   How many naps should your baby be getting? _____
   How many naps is your baby getting *now*? _____
   How many hours should your baby be napping? _____
   How many hours is your baby napping *now*? _____
2. Do you have a formal nap routine? _____
3. Are you watching for sleepy signs and putting your baby down for a nap as soon as you notice he's tired? _____
4. Are your baby's naptimes/lengths consistent every day? _____

Ten-Day Prebedtime Routine Log

Baby's Name: _____

Age: _____

Date: _____

How many days have you been following your plan? _____

Key:
Activity: active, moderate, or calm
Noise: loud, moderate, or quiet
Light: bright, dim, or dark

Time	What we did	Activity level	Noise level	Light level

1. For the past ten days, approximately how many days did you follow your formal bedtime routine? _____

2. Is the hour prior to bedtime mostly peaceful, quiet, and dimly lit? _____

3. Does your bedtime routine help your baby wind down and prepare for sleep? _____

4. Is your nightly routine consistent, acting as a bedtime cue for your baby? _____

5. Is your bedtime routine relaxing and enjoyable for you? _____

Ten-Day Night-Waking Log

Baby's Name: _____

Age: _____

Date: _____

How many days have you been following your plan? _____

Time	How baby woke me up	How long awake; what we did	Time baby fell back to sleep	How baby fell back to sleep	How long of a sleep stretch since fell asleep

Asleep time: _____

Awake time: _____

Total number of awakenings: _____

Longest sleep span: _____

Total hours of sleep: _____

This is a comparison of your logs. Fill in the times and the amount of change:

	First log	Ten days	Amount of change	Twenty days	Amount of change	Thirty days	Amount of change	Forty days	Amount of change
Number of naps									
Length of naps									
Bedtime: Asleep time									
Awake time									
Number of awakenings									
Longest sleep span									
Total hours of sleep									

Use this worksheet to examine your experience every ten days:

During the past ten days, how closely did you follow your plan?

☐ I followed all parts of my plan exactly for all ten days.

☐ I followed some parts of my plan, but not everything.

☐ I started out great, but reverted back to my old habits.

☐ Plan? What plan? (Oops, better start over with Step One!)

Have you seen positive changes in at least one area (for example: a fifteen-minute increase in naptime or sleep span; an earlier bedtime; a reduction in the number of night wakings)? _____

What areas show the most change? _____

Why do you think that's true? (What have you done to influence this?) _____

_____

_____

_____

What areas show the least change? _____

Why do you think that's true? (What have you done to influence this?) _____

_____

_____

_____

_____

What have you learned about your baby's sleep habits over the past ten days? _____

_____

_____

_____

_____

_____

What parts of your plan seem to be having the best influence on your baby's sleep? _____

_____

_____

What changes do you think you now need to make? _____

_____

_____

_____

How are you going to make these changes? _____

_____

_____

_____

Part II

Let's Talk About You

Your baby isn't sleeping all night, yet somehow he wakes up cheerfully and bounces through his days with a joyful exuberance about life that belies any lack of shut-eye. You, on the other hand, may find yourself wandering about aimlessly in a sleep-deprived stupor, longing for that seemingly impossible night when you can stay snuggled in your bed—all night—without interruption. Even worse, you may be waking up on your own in between the baby's stirrings, adding to an already frustrating situation. Many parents find that once their baby is sleeping soundly, they continue their *own* pattern of frequent night waking. If there's anything more challenging than waking for your baby every few hours, it's waking every few hours even when your baby is sleeping peacefully!

This section is about *you*. It's about helping you to get back to a normal pattern of sleep. And it's full of good news: By following these tips, you should be snoozing happily in no time.

The final chapter in this book is about keeping your sanity during this sleepless time. It will nudge you along in your journey toward balance and help you stay focused on the future. It will give you ways to ease your frustration and helplessness and strengthen your resolve to work through your baby's, and your own, sleep plans right now.

11

Baby's Sleeping (Finally!) but Mommy's Not

After following the No-Cry Sleep Solution—making your sleep plan, charting your progress, persevering night after night—your baby is finally sleeping. It's incredible. It's wonderful. All is well with the sandman in your house. Your baby is sleeping through the night.

But *you* aren't.

Mother-Speak

"The baby's sleeping all night but I'm up every two hours staring at the clock."

Robin, mother of thirteen-month-old Alicia

Take heart: This is a very common situation, and this chapter will tell you how to improve your own sleep.

What's Happening?

A few things in the past year or more have disrupted your sleep. Things like pregnancy, followed by a baby, and perhaps followed by another pregnancy, and one or more additional babies. If your baby joined your family by adoption, you've lost sleep throughout the long and involved process, and then through the early months of baby sleeplessness.

You may not realize that you've actually gotten into the *habit* of waking up during the night. Your *normal* night's sleep includes many night wakings, and your system has become accustomed to a certain level of sleep deprivation.

It's probably been a long time since you've really had a full night's sleep. Almost certainly even longer than you realize! Many parents actually forget what their sleep patterns were like before children entered their lives. Many assume that they used to get eight hours consistently and without interruption. Eight hours *is* the amount of time that sleep experts recommend for most adults. In reality, though, according to the National Sleep Foundation, adults sleep an average of about seven hours per night. Furthermore, at least half of all adults have trouble sleeping—falling asleep and staying asleep—baby or no baby. In other words, if you weren't sleeping like a log before baby, you won't be sleeping like a log now, either.

There's another aspect to your current sleep situation to consider. As we age (and you've been doing that over the past few years, you know), the amount of sleep we need and the amount of sleep we get tend to decline, and sleep problems increase.

Recent studies by the National Sleep Foundation have acknowledged the impact of the ebb and flow of monthly hormones on our sleep. In their studies, 43 percent of women reported disturbed sleep during the week *before* their period; 71 percent reported sleep problems *during* their period. In addition, 79 percent of women reported sleep problems during pregnancy. (Personally, I think this figure is far too low—probably because the 21 percent who checked the "no" box in this poll were just too tired to understand the question.)

According to sleep experts, it's not only age, but also the stresses of adult life that contribute to our sleep problems. (Plus, I hate to be the bearer of bad news, but you have something even more to look forward to. An estimated 50 to 90 percent of people older than sixty have sleep problems.)

Add all of these situations together and there are very few nights when our sleep is not disrupted for some reason.

So, now you know *the rest of the story.* You can't blame *all* your nighttime problems on parenthood!

How to Get a Good Night's Sleep

Because you've just experienced a period of frequent night waking, I don't have to tell you that the quality and quantity of your sleep can affect your entire life. Getting adequate, restful sleep is essential to your health and well being.

Everyone has different sleep needs, and you should gauge your sleep requirements according to your own health. Let your own body tell you what it needs, and do your best to listen to it. Learn to recognize the signs that tell you that you are or are not getting enough sleep.

The following are a few helpful tips for improving adult sleep that I've run across in my exhaustive research for this book. Sift through the list and use as many as you wish. Applying even just one or two of these suggestions should prove helpful.

Here's an important point to bear in mind. Sometimes, people who have been sleep deprived for any length of time actually feel *more* tired when they first begin to make changes to improve their sleep rhythms. The good news is that this is short-lived, and as soon as you adjust to your improved sleep, you will feel better emotionally and physically.

Review the following ideas, check off the ones that appeal to you, and create your *own* sleep plan. Soon, you'll be sleeping— like a baby (a baby who *doesn't* wake up every two hours).

Stop Worrying About Sleep

It's fantastic that your baby is sleeping better now. That was the goal when you bought this book and you've already had your success. It's just a matter of time before you are sleeping better, as well—once you're accustomed to your baby's new routine and sure that he is, too. The cruel irony is that lying in bed worrying because you can't fall or stay asleep will just keep you awake! So, relax. Follow these suggestions and sleep will come.

Turn your clock away from your bed, and don't agonize over whether you are sleeping or not. You can't force yourself to sleep by fretting about it. The best you can do is to establish good sleeping habits and follow them nightly.

As a busy parent, you may be compounding your problem by worrying that your sleep time is taking up productive time that could be spent doing other things. You either get yourself to bed much too late, or lie in bed and feel guilty about it, thinking about all those other things you "should" be doing. Give yourself permission to sleep. It's necessary for your body, important for your health, and good for your soul. Remember that your baby will benefit if you are well rested, too, because you'll be a happier Mommy (or Daddy). And if you're breastfeeding or pregnant your improved sleep will be beneficial to both you and your baby.

Pay Off Your Sleep Debt

When we don't get enough sleep, we create a sleep debt that mounts further with each additional sleepless night. If you are still feeling sleep-deprived, try to gather as many additional sleep minutes as you can. Set aside two weeks to squeeze in some extra sleep. Make it a priority. Go to bed early whenever possible, take a nap when you can, sleep a few minutes later. Even an extra hour of sleep will help you to pay off at least a portion of your sleep debt. You'll feel much better and can move on to establishing a healthy sleep routine.

If you simply cannot find any time for extra sleep, then bypass this idea and work on developing a healthy sleep routine. You may find that it will take a month or so for your sleep debt to dissipate and your new sleep program to work, but it will. Once you've developed your own plan, you'll find that sleep will no longer be on your list of things to think about. It will instead be just a simple, natural part of your life, the way it is for your baby.

Set Your Body Clock

Your body has what amounts to an internal alarm clock that can be set for sleep time and awake time. The consistency of your sleep schedule sets this clock and makes it work for you. If your bedtime and awake time are different every day, the effectiveness of this amazing gift of nature is undermined; your clock is out of sync. You'll find yourself tired or alert at inappropriate times, sometimes feeling as if you could fall asleep standing up during the day, but then lying wide awake in bed at night.

This explains why many people have trouble waking up on Monday morning. If you have a specific wake and sleep time during the week, you probably find that by Friday morning you are waking up just before your alarm goes off, and on Friday night it's an effort to stay awake during the late-night movie. Come Monday morning, you're groggy and exhausted when your morning alarm goes off. What has happened is that by the end of the week your biological clock has taken control because of your consistent wake-sleep schedule during the week. But come the weekend, we push our bedtimes later, and, if we're lucky enough to manage it, we sleep late in the morning as well. This effectively cancels the setting on our clocks, and by Monday we have to start all over again.

This imbalance is an easy one to fix—and a solid, consistent sleep plan is the handy tool that will do the trick. Choose a specific bedtime and time to wake up; stick to it as closely as possible, seven days a week. Obviously, your busy life will alter this routine sometimes. You can deviate from your plan once in a while without doing too much to upset things. But on the whole, if you adhere to your schedule as consistently as possible, your sleep will be more refreshing, and you'll be more energetic and alert. Your body clock will function as it should, allowing you to tick through your day productively and wind down at night calmly.

Naturally, a few lucky people can function perfectly with a varying sleep schedule, but they're the exception. Most people are helped immensely by this simple, effective suggestion.

Get Organized

When your days are hectic and disorganized, your stress level increases; the natural physiological and emotional responses to this stress hamper your ability to sleep. So we can attack this kind of sleeplessness by getting at the root of it—becoming more organized and purposeful during the day.

A formal daily to-do list or calendar can help you feel more in control of your days. With the myriad critical details of each day written down, you'll be able to relax somewhat. Think of it as moving all the dates and times and tasks out of your head and onto paper, freeing up a little breathing room upstairs. And late at night you won't wonder, "What do I need to do? What did I forget?" It's all right there in your lists and on your calendar. Keep a pad and a pencil near your bed in case an important idea or task *does* pop into your mind as you're trying to drift off. Write it down—then *let it go for now.*

Avoid Caffeine Late in the Day

Here's an interesting tidbit. Caffeine stays in your bloodstream between six and fourteen hours! The caffeine in that after-dinner cup of coffee is still hanging around in your system at midnight and beyond. Caffeine contains a chemical that causes hyperactivity and wakefulness, which is why many people find their morning coffee so stimulating. Tolerance levels for caffeine vary; so you'll need to experiment and find out how much you can drink and how late you can drink it without disrupting your sleep.

If you are a nursing mother, watch your baby carefully to see if she too is being affected by caffeine. While no study has proved the connection between caffeine and a baby's sleeplessness, we do know that diet affects the quality, quantity, and palatability of breast milk, so a connection is not exactly farfetched. (Many a breastfeeding mother has reported a perceived effect of caffeine on her baby, so it's worth taking a look at your own situation.)

Keep in mind that caffeine is an ingredient in more than just coffee. Tea (green as well as black), cola, some other soft drinks (even root beer and orange; check the labels), chocolate, even some over-the-counter painkillers contain it, although in smaller amounts.

Better choices for prebed drinks are warm milk or herbal teas that will bring on the relaxed state needed for sleep.

Watch Out for the Effects of Drugs and Alcohol

If you are taking any medication, ask your doctor or pharmacist if it has any side effects. We often are aware of what medications make us drowsy, but we don't realize that some have the opposite effect—acting as a stimulant.

Likewise, an evening glass or two of wine or beer usually won't affect sleep and might bring it on. But more than that can have a rebound effect, causing an episode of insomnia a few hours later, in the middle of the night. Alcohol can also disturb the *quality* of your sleep, making it shallow and disrupting normal dream cycles.

Make Exercise a Part of Your Day

There are many benefits to fitting regular exercise into your day, and improved sleep is at the top of the list. Many studies (not to mention common, everyday experience) have shown that moderate, regular exercise reduces insomnia and improves the quality of sleep.

The key to using exercise to improve sleep is to maintain a regular pattern: thirty to forty-five minutes of moderate aerobic exercise, three to four times a week. For best results, make sure you complete your exercise at least three hours before bedtime; exercise leaves most people too energized for sleep right after. (Once again, there are exceptions. Some people find that strenuous exercise helps them fall asleep quickly soon afterward. Experiment to learn if this applies to you.)

You might think your baby precludes your ability to get out and exercise. On the contrary! Your baby gives you the perfect excuse for a daily walk behind the stroller. If winter weather gets in your way, head for an indoor shopping mall with room to roam. This may not work for you every day, and you may have to leave your wallet at home, but many parents find it an effective way to squeeze in a walk. Plus, most babies love it and benefit from the stimulation (which may in fact help baby sleep, too).

Here are a few other ways to incorporate daily exercise into your life:

If you work at home:

- After you put your little one down for a nap, use a treadmill, stationary bike, or other gym equipment.
- Jog up and down your stairs.
- Bring your baby outside and do some gardening.

If you work outside the home:

- At lunchtime or during a break, climb up and down the stairs, or take a walk around the block.
- Create a routine to take advantage of an employee gym or workout room.
- Take frequent brisk walks to the copy machine, mail room, or bathroom.

Ideas for everyone:

- Play an exercise video and exercise with your baby.
- Put on some great music and dance with your baby.
- Look for small ways to add exercise into your day such as parking farther away from the store, using the stairs instead of the elevator, walking instead of driving to a close destination, walking your older kids to school, or playing outside with your children.
- Plan family activities that involve movement and action, such as hikes, bike rides, or romps at the beach or park.

Make Your Environment Favorable to Sleep

Take a good look at your bedroom and make sure that it is conducive to relaxation and healthy sleep. Every person is different, but here's a checklist for you to review.

- **Comfort.** Is your mattress comfortable to you? Does it provide the amount of support that you need? Do you like your blanket or comforter, or is it a source of aggravation in the night? Is your pillow the right softness and thickness? Do you find its material cozy and soothing? Do what you can to improve these details.
- **Temperature.** If you are too cold or too hot during sleep, you will wake frequently. Experiment until you find the best temperature. If your partner has different preferences, find a way to please both of you by changing the type of pajamas you wear, using a fan, or piling on extra blankets.
- **Noise.** Some people sleep better in perfect silence, while others prefer background music or white noise. Again, if one sleep partner likes noise, but the other wants silence, experiment: Try earplugs or a personal headset for music or sound.
- **Light.** If you sleep better in complete darkness, cover your windows. If you like light, open the blinds, or use a nightlight. (Be cautious about using lights during the night if you wake up to use the bathroom or tend the baby. Bright light will fool your biological clock into thinking it's morning. Rely on low-wattage night-lights.) Here again, if your partner likes the blinds open and you like them shut, decide whose needs are greater or find a compromise. You might buy yourself a soft eye mask made just for that purpose, or leave the blinds open on one side of the room, closed on the other—facing the closed window will give you more of a sense of darkness.

Have Your Own Bedtime Routine

You may have implemented a bedtime routine to help your baby sleep better. This same idea can work for you, too. Often, we parents have a very pleasant routine for putting our children to bed.

After that relaxing hour, when we have just about fallen to sleep reading the bedtime story, we jam into high gear and rush about the house tending to all those duties that await our attention until we look up and—oh no! It's midnight!

Your own prebedtime routine can greatly improve your ability to fall asleep and stay asleep. It can include anything that relaxes you, such as reading; listening to music; or sitting with your spouse, sipping a cup of tea, and talking. Avoid stimulating your mind or body in the hour before bed. Tasks like answering your E-mail, doing heavy housecleaning, or watching television can keep you awake long after you've finished them.

If possible, try to keep the lights dim in the hour before bed, as bright light strongly signals your body to leap into daytime action. Lower lights and quieter sounds will help prepare you for a good night's sleep.

Eat Right and Eat Light Before Sleep

You will sleep best with your stomach neither too full nor too empty. A large meal can make you feel tired but will keep your body working to digest it, thus disturbing sleep. An empty stomach can keep you up with hunger pains. A happy medium is usually best. Have a light snack about an hour or two before bedtime. Avoid gassy, fatty, sugary, or spicy foods. Some foods that have been found to help people sleep better are milk, eggs, cottage cheese, turkey, and cashews. Experiment to find which choices are best for you.

Encourage Relaxation and the Onset of Sleep

Often, when we lay in bed waiting for sleep, our mind and body are primed for action. The wheels are turning and our thoughts keep us awake. A helpful method for bringing on sleep is to focus your mind on peaceful, relaxing thoughts. Here are a few ways to accomplish this:

- Repeat a familiar meditation or prayer to release the mind from daily action and prime it for sleep. Yoga stretches can help relax your muscles.
- Focus on your breathing while repeating the word *relax* in a slow pattern tied to your exhales. Or imagine your breathing is moving in and out along with a wave at the beach.
- Use progressive relaxation to coax all the parts of your body to relax. Begin at your feet. Feel the weight of your feet, have them go limp and relaxed, and then imagine that they have a gentle warmth moving over them. Then, move up to your right leg, repeat the process. Move on to your left leg, and continue on up to your head. (Most people are asleep or nearly asleep by the time they get that far!) You may want to adapt some of the relaxation exercises you learned in childbirth classes.

When Engorgement Is the Problem

There is often an adjustment period when a breastfed baby begins to sleep through the night. It's hard to believe, but your breasts *will* develop their own clock system. Decreased production during the night is quite normal, and within a week of your baby's new sleep habits, your milk production pattern will parallel your baby's new feeding pattern. Your breasts will still produce milk constantly, so if your baby wakes once in a while to nurse, he'll find enough there for comfort. Interestingly enough, if your baby suddenly begins to wake again because of teething, illness, or growth spurts, your milk production will shift right along with his needs (as long as you feed on demand). What a great miracle breastfeeding is!

Mother-Speak

"Last night we had our best sleep night ever—my little guy slept seven whole hours. The problem is that I woke up in the middle of the night with rocks on my chest! My breasts were leaking, and they hurt. After working so hard to get him to sleep, I didn't dare wake him up. I've so longed for the time my baby would sleep through the night—I never dreamed I would wish he would wake up to nurse!"

Elisa, mother of nine-month-old Jahwill

Adjustment Period Solutions

Here are a few tips for getting through the adjustment period.

- Give your baby a complete, both-sides feeding before bed and in the morning.
- Sleep in your roomiest bra with nursing pads or washcloths tucked inside.
- If you wake engorged, apply warm compresses and pump a small amount (either by hand or with a breast pump). Don't pump a full feeding because you'll trick your body into thinking baby is still needing that nighttime feeding. Just release enough to get comfortable.
- Try taking a warm shower and massaging your breasts under the spray of water. You might want to lean forward so that gravity helps you to express some milk. This may help you release enough milk to get comfortable until your baby wakes up to nurse.
- Apply a cold compress to your breasts, or use ibuprofen to minimize any pain or discomfort.
- If you are in pain and cannot pump, go ahead—pick up your sleeping baby and put him to your breast. Most babies

can nurse in their sleep, and yours may suck just enough to help you get back to sleep. Even if your baby wakes during this feeding, he'll fall right back to sleep easily during the nursing session.

- Be prepared for additional daytime feedings for a bit. Some babies who suddenly begin sleeping longer at night will make up for the lost feedings by nursing more during the day.
- If you have experienced plugged ducts or breast infections in the past, avoid any repeats by pumping or nursing your baby enough to soften your breasts. Just try to minimize this so that you can work the nighttime feeding out of your schedule. Remember that your body will adjust production to match your baby's new sleep schedule.
- Don't stop breastfeeding! Your breasts still need to be emptied, and frequent daytime feeding will help you move past this uncomfortable condition.

Pay Attention to Your Own Health

If you have chronic insomnia or other unusual sleep problems, or other health problems, be smart. See a doctor.

12

Final Thoughts: Mom-to-Mom

As I finish up this book, I am thinking about how far I've come with Coleton's sleep habits. When my journey first began, he was twelve months old and waking every hour to nurse. The desperate longing for sleep filled my nights; a frantic and relentless search through books and on the Internet for something—anything—that would help Coleton sleep consumed my days. Through it all, though, one criterion guided me. Whatever ideas I tried, I would not allow my baby to cry himself to sleep. After all, we were in the same boat: We both needed sleep and couldn't figure out how to make it happen.

That's not to say that my tears didn't threaten occasionally. I remember nights when he woke me for the sixth time and I prayed, "Please, God, just let him sleep." Like you, my readers and friends, I learned that when one is deprived of sleep, sleep becomes the absolute priority in life.

Now that I'm standing on the other side of the bridge (or shall I say, bed?), sleep is no longer a major issue in my life. Coleton routinely takes a two-hour nap and sleeps all night with few disruptions. On the occasion when he does wake to nurse, I'm well rested and able to handle his midnight call without distress. Sleep has once again become a simple matter of maintenance in our home.

My test moms followed the same path. They began the trip with bags under their eyes and anguished pleas for help:

Mothers-Speak

"I hate to say it, but I have become obsessed with sleep."

Caryn, mother of six-month-old Blaine

"By morning, I'm a walking zombie. I'd do anything for a full night's sleep; it's become my ultimate obsession."

Yelena, mother of seven-month-old Samantha

"I am ALWAYS exhausted. I walk around all day in a fog. I really, really can't let my baby cry, but I really, really want sleep."

Neela, mother of eighteen-month-old Abhishek

These mothers ended their journey revitalized and ready to move forward to the next milestone in their baby's lives:

Mothers-Speak

"I'm amazed at how far we've come. I can't believe this is the same baby. I feel like a new mother. A happy, energetic mother who sleeps all night and wakes up refreshed and joyful."

Robin, mother of thirteen-month-old Alicia

"Josh now goes gracefully to bed almost every single night. And I have the whole evening to work, take a shower, eat dinner, fix his lunch for day care. It's like having two days in one."

Shannon, mother of nineteen-month-old Joshua

"Kailee is in bed every night by 8:00 P.M., and the earliest I ever hear from her is 6:30 A.M. It has totally changed our lives. It's a new freedom that we enjoy wholeheartedly."

Marsha, mother of eight-month-old Kailee

We Are Alike

As I worked with my group of test mommies, I discovered how alike we all are. Different names, different places, but the same heart. We love our babies absolutely; we can't bear to hear them cry, nor can we easily tolerate the cries of other babies. Our lives were irrevocably and completely changed the minute the pregnancy test came up positive. And as our babies grow, the special place in our hearts reserved just for them grows bigger, too.

We also have strong opinions about parenting and are not easily swayed by the media, our friends, or even our pediatricians or other "experts." We know in our hearts what our babies need; we feel what they want. Blessed by, and mindful of, advances in medicine, and wary of philosophies developed in the interest of convenience, we are determined to heed our strong instincts. We are even willing to suffer ourselves, if it means the best for our babies. We are mother lions, mother bears, and father tigers, too. We parent by heart.

If You've Just Begun

If you have just embarked on this journey toward better sleep, I know that you are frustrated and anxious. Because you are determined not to let your baby cry, I know that the feedback you get from family, friends, and possibly even your pediatrician isn't always helpful or supportive.

Talking with others who share your parenting philosophies really does help. If you are lucky enough to find someone nearby who believes as you do, make sure that you both take advantage of this by talking to each other frequently. If you don't have a local friend, you can find support via the Internet. Many parenting websites have posting boards or chats where you can find like-minded parents. Helpful websites abound, offering information,

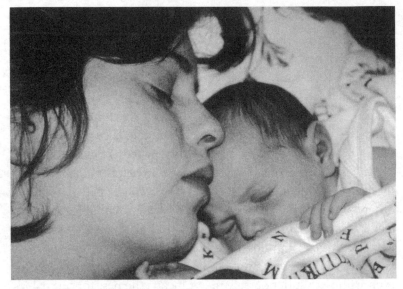

Jill and Kate, two weeks old

articles, message boards, chat rooms, and more. Some I've found quite helpful include:

babiestoday.com
babycenter.com
babyzone.com
breastfeeding.com
geoparent.com
mothering.com
myria.com
nursingbaby.com
parenthoodweb.com
parentsoup.com
parentsplace.com
storknet.com

You may find that having someone to talk to—either in person, by phone, or by computer—can mean the difference between depression and commitment. I encourage you to find the support you need to help yourself through this challenging time.

Living for the Moment?

As your sleep issues cast lengthening shadows over your life, you may begin to live purely for the moment. Your sleep-deprived, foggy brain may focus so intently on sleep that you can't think beyond the next few hours of rest. What you lack is perspective. To gain it back, ask yourself these questions:

1. Where will I be five years from now?
2. How will I look back on this time?
3. Will I be proud of how I handled my baby's sleep routines, or will I regret my actions?
4. How will the things I do with my baby today affect the person he will become in the future?

I know I've said this already, but having older children has afforded me the perspective I lacked the first time around. My children have taught me how very quickly babyhood passes. I struggle now to remember the difficulties of those first couple years, as they are so fleeting. And I am proud that I didn't cave in to the pressures of others around us; instead following my heart as I gently nurtured all of my babies. That time has passed for us, but those memories remain.

I look upon my older children and I like what I see. They are kind, sensitive, and caring young people, and I've tried very hard to instill solid values. Yet, they are still young enough—so much closer to the essence of humanity—to react without thought, on an instinctual level, to certain situations. Watching them has reinforced what I suspected but what adult logic often obscures. When their baby brother cries, all three of them run to his aid. When one of the three is hurt, the others offer an ice pack, a soothing word, or a hug. From the depths of their unjaded souls, they cringe when they see a parent ignore a wailing baby.

My kids know what to do in part because it hasn't been very long since they were babies themselves. They can still relate to the desperation of a baby's cry. It's simple for them because they're free of adult baggage and clutter: When a baby cries, the right response is, well, *response*. It's just that simple.

It's not *all* instinct, however; I believe that my commitment to handling all my babies gently—my refusal to let them cry it out—has contributed to the sensitive people they are today. Of course, it wasn't always easy. Attaining anything of true value rarely is.

Baseball Babies

My three older children all play baseball, so Coleton and I spend much of our springtime at the ballpark. His first baseball season he was five months old. Since I was a coach on my daughter's team, Coleton spent his time in the dugout and on the field nestled in his sling, watching the action and listening to the cheers, chants, and noise of the play. Between swings at bat the girls would often pass him around from one to the other, entertaining him and trying to make him giggle. That same season I met another mother with a baby boy the same age as Coleton. She always arrived with her little son belted into his car seat–stroller travel system. There he would remain, parked at the edge of the bleachers. His reclining position in the seat gave him a view of the sky and trees. When he fussed, his mother would prop a bottle in his seat, and he would drink until he fell asleep. As I chatted with this other mother, as baseball moms do, I discovered the difference extended beyond the field. While Coleton's nights were spent sleeping with his Mommy by his side, nursing whenever he felt the need for comfort, the other mother was practicing sleep training—putting her baby in his crib at bedtime and ignoring his cries until the appropriate morning hour, "teaching" him to "self soothe" himself to sleep.

Both Coleton and this other baby were quiet babies. Rarely would you hear either one of them cry. But, as I contemplated the lives of these children, I wondered how their early experiences would color their futures. Coleton's early life was filled with people—their warm arms, happy faces, cuddles, and touches. He was always in the middle of life, not only enjoying his own experiences but also observing the experiences of others. His nights were no different than his days: someone was always there to heed his call. This other baby's early months were spent strapped in his stroller, hearing people, but from an uninvolved distance except for the occasional visitor who leaned over his seat. His nights were vast hours of loneliness, his cries ignored.

Coleton's early life was filled with the golden communication of humanity, where he will most likely search to be as he grows. The other baby was shown independence and aloneness during the first part of his life. Yes, they both may have been content babies, but content with entirely different worlds—one that was people-centered and one revolving around separateness from people. I find myself wondering: how will these early experiences color the men these babies will become? As you move through these early months with *your* baby, take the time to consider how today's actions will affect your child in the long run. This process will help you toss off unhelpful advice as you work through your own sleep solutions.

Patience, Patience, and Just a Little More Patience

Take a deep breath and repeat after me, "This too shall pass." You're in the middle of it all right now, and it's hard. But in no time at all, your baby will be sleeping, and so will you. And your concerns will turn to the next phase in this magnificent, challenging, and ultimately rewarding experience we call parenthood. I wish you and your family a lifetime of happiness and love.

For More Information

You can read interviews with many of the original test mommies at the author's website: www.pantley.com.

To obtain a free catalog of parenting books, videos, audiotapes, and newsletters; or information about lecture services available by Elizabeth Pantley; or to contact the author:

Write to the author at:
5720 127th Avenue NE
Kirkland, WA 98033-8741

E-mail the author at:
elizabeth@pantley.com

Call the toll-free order line:
800-422-5820

Fax your request:
425-828-4833

Visit the website:
pantley.com

Search the Internet for articles by "Elizabeth Pantley"

Index

About the Author

Parenting educator Elizabeth Pantley is president of Better Beginnings, Inc., a family resource and education company. Elizabeth frequently speaks to parents in schools, hospitals, and parent groups, and her presentations are received with enthusiasm and praise.

She is a regular radio show guest and frequently quoted as a parenting expert in magazines such as *Parents, Parenting, Working Mother, Woman's Day, Good Housekeeping, McCalls,* and *Redbook* and on more than fifty parent-directed websites. She publishes a newsletter, *Parent Tips,* that is distributed in schools nationwide, and she is the author of three previous parenting books:

- *Hidden Messages: What Our Words and Actions Are Really Telling Our Children*
- *Perfect Parenting: The Dictionary of 1,000 Parenting Tips*
- *Kid Cooperation: How to Stop Yelling, Nagging and Pleading & Get Kids to Cooperate*

Her most recent credits include *The Successful Child: What Parents Can Do to Help Kids Turn Out Well* (Little, Brown and Company), a joint effort with Dr. William and Martha Sears.

She and her husband, Robert, live in the state of Washington with their four children, Grama (Elizabeth's mother), and assorted family pets. She is an involved participant in her children's school and sports activities and has served in positions as varied as softball coach and school PTA president.

All four of her children sleep through the night.

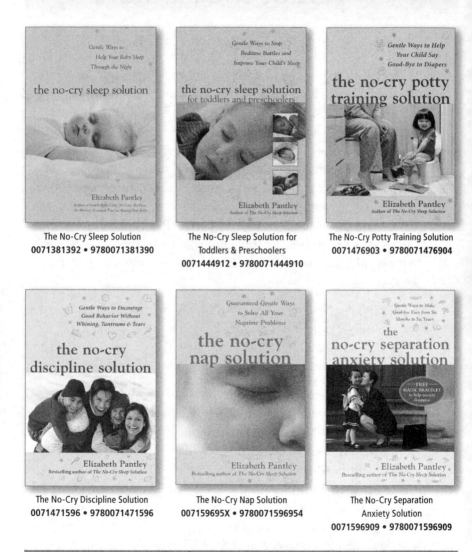